Exiled in Paradise

By J.F. "Smitty" Smith

Published by J.F. Smith

New Orleans, LA

Exiled in Paradise

Copyright © 2012 by J.F. Smith

Cover & text design by Hannah Adams

ISBN-13: 978-1478260219
ISBN-10: 1478260211

DEDICATED TO

The Spears & the McFaddens.

The families I never got to know.

Table of Contents

I think the most important stories are those that illuminate patterns throughout history, that open our eyes to connections, repetitions and trends between our past and present experiences.

Exiled in Paradise is such a story. As Smitty recollects his experiences in the seven tumultuous days following Hurricane Katrina and the federal levee breaches, he contextualizes the event within a historic context of white supremacy, through stories of slavery, Jim Crow and urban renewal/removal. He acts as a voice box for members of his family and community whose testimonies contribute to his multi-generational chronicle. And he connects stories of community organizing after Katrina to a legacy of resistance to racial injustice.

Smitty is a writer, a historian, an organizer, an artist, a scholar, a community leader, an entrepreneur, and a dear, dear friend. It has been a great honor to work with him on this manuscript for the past couple of years. I am confident that you will learn as much from his journey as I have.

-Hannah Adams, *July 2012*

Our presentation of some of the situations we encountered during Hurricane Katrina spans a timeline of seven days. The evacuation began Sunday, August 28th, from my house in the Lower 9th Ward, and ended late Saturday night, September 3rd, at Windsor Ward Mall near Kelly Air Force Base in San Antonio, Texas.

As the hurricane approached from those distant waters, the mayor announced that there was no immediate emergency but a voluntary evacuation advisory order had been put in place. The news came that the hurricane was on track to hit New Orleans. The mayor issued a second order that the city was now under a mandatory evacuation order and everyone had to evacuate. Even as the storm threatened the city, the mandatory evacuation order was reversed. Finally, the mayor issued an absolute mandatory order. Everyone had to leave the city or be arrested under the law. The city was in complete disarray, most people were scrambling to get to safe, high ground. The only plans the city issued were "Get out, and get out now." The state claimed it had a plan in place.

During this process it appeared the mayor had abandoned the city, the state reversed its evacuation order, and the Federal Government remained indifferent to the needs of the people in distress.

Something happened during this hurricane like no other. The hurricane and its aftermath took several turns for the worst. As the storm approached, the winds hit the city fast and furious. Canals were breached, the floodwater rose to historic heights, lives were lost, and property damage reached unprecedented levels. The repeated requests for emergency assistance from the state and federal governments were sent to various agencies, never to be heard from again.

One of the largest displacement of people in the history of the country was now in full bloom. These helpless people, the children, the elderly, the sick, and all others who were in dire need and unable to fend for themselves, were delivered into the jaws of these unforgiving destructive forces by the inaction of the authorities.

As we were evacuated from one place to another, within the city fear and panic were beginning to evidence themselves in the faces and behaviors of the people. These frightening situations seemed to produce explosive conversations, which were everywhere. There were bad encounters with conspiracy advocates who were pushing their theories all over the place to anyone who would bend to their demands.

However, it appeared the most sober conversations came from those evacuees with an overarching belief that the Black people's predicament is deeply rooted in the historical relationship between the government (the White Ruling Class) and the poverty-stricken Black population.

The constant talk we heard was that the White Ruling Class of New Orleans had laid plans long ago to reduce the majority Black population to a manageable political minority. These evacuees often referred to themselves and all the other displaced as "refugees." They strongly supported the notion that Katrina had created the perfect conditions under which the Ruling Class would continue their plan of dismantling the Black community.

This writing emanated out of the many conversations with these groups and other displaced people about their historical relationship with the Ruling Class. In addition, we attempted to ascertain whether the evacuees'/refugees' claims of disenfranchisement had historical roots or whether such maltreatments were a mere accident of history. We also looked at situations far and near and at various aspects of that relationship in an attempt to arrive at an understanding of the direction in which this relationship was headed.

No attempt has been made hereunder to delineate or reconcile all of the problems deeply embedded in this unusual historical relationship. Any particular conclusion deduced herefrom rests solely with the reader. However, some of our observations are herein contained.

Somewhere up way up high, above those magnificent white clouds, on the other side of space and time, deep, deep beyond the heart of the heavens, there is a place called the Land of Paradise where people like you and me will forever be free.

-*Aunt Martha's Slave Journal; 1860*

TIMELINE

Day 1: Sunday, August 28, 2005

THE JOURNEY BEGINS

1. Leaving the Lower 9th Ward

Day 2: Monday, August 29, 2005

THE STORM

2. The Storm Moves On

Day 3: Tuesday, August 30, 2005

DAY OF NO RETURN

3. Leaving

4. The Parking Lot: Our Home

5. One Little Girl

6. Faded Dreams

7. Miss Agness

Day 4: Wednesday, August 31, 2005

Day 5: Thursday, September 1, 2005

Day 6: Friday, September 2, 2005

Day 7: Saturday, September 3, 2005

THE ENDLESS JOURNEY

35. Rastafarians Defy the Military

36. The Community-Based Group

37. Our Shattered Dreams

38. The Lost Brother

39. The Endless Journey

After spending some time on the streets of New Orleans, we finally arrived at the Convention Center, unknown to us, the end point of our journey through the city.

The Center was the centerpiece of most of the activities and of this writing.

The Superdome was basically outside the scope of this writing. We didn't have an on-site presence at that venue, and any mention thereof is included herein by reference to those who were there.

EXILED IN PARADISE

I was born in darkness and have lived in darkness all my days. I am looking and hoping to see the bright lights of freedom before I leave this land of darkness. I have grown old and weary; my duty is done. If I can just see a glimmer of hope I don't have to see the daybreak and I don't have to see the sun. But I would be forever thankful if I could just see some of the darkness fade away, I would know that freedom is on its way.

-From the Slave Journal

Day 1: Sunday, August 28, 2005

1. Leaving the Lower 9th Ward

LEAVING THE LOWER 9TH WARD

Friends calling from New York and California informed me of the impending storm and the need to leave. Cousin Pam called early Sunday morning and offered her apartment. Friends were satisfied that I had a place to go.

Pam and her daughter Michelle arrived about 3:00 PM, yet I had not packed anything for an extended stay. With a medium sized bag, my favorite blanket, a backpack, and a few books for overnight reading, we were off to Pam's apartment for an overnight stay or two.

On our way, we made several stops for extended periods of time at homes of her friends, as I waited in my vehicle. I was not privy to the conversations nor did I make any inquiry into the nature of her visits.

Pam and her daughter occupied an apartment on the second floor in an upscale neighborhood in New Orleans East. We arrived just after dark and immediately began to remove all items from the porch that could cause damage to the property. Before too long we had secured the property from the distant yet oncoming winds.

We talked about family matters and about some of the people we knew into the early morning. At one point

Pam looked over at me in a perturbing kind of way and asked, "Why didn't you stay home and help out the family instead of running off to all those different places?" Before I could answer she jumped in with, "What was so great about Chicago and Los Angeles in those days anyway? So New Orleans wasn't good enough for you?"

"Pam, you have to realize that New Orleans was a very segregated city in those days," I said. "Jobs were not easy to come by for whites, let alone for Blacks. What few jobs were made available to us were mostly allocated to the so-called 'Negro Establishment.' Most of us in the Lower 9th Ward had no claim of birthright to that socioeconomic order.

"Back then there was no real progressive movement anywhere in the city. However, like many of our young students, I too joined the Youth Council of the NAACP. Whatever contact we had with young white radical political groups was pursued cautiously, and in a somewhat clandestine kind of way. Any youth movement, regardless of its politics, was considered by the white establishment to be some kind of communist front organization. Most of us concluded there was no real vision for us in the pursuit of freedom and social justice in the entire city."

I continued. "I opted for Chicago over Los Angeles. The Windy City, as always, had a very large transplanted

Black population from New Orleans. I had traveled to Chicago the two previous summers prior to graduation and friends had encouraged the relocation. Chicago was a great city, probably still is, and I became fully engaged. The only drawback to this wonderful city was the winter and the wind (the 'Hawk of Lake Michigan' as it was called.) The day I headed west it was about 23 below zero. Farewell Chicago, I thought. It's time to move on."

The feeling came to me that my cousin was not quite through with her polite but persistent probe into my life.

Soon the news came that devastating winds had the state under siege. The city had been abandoned to these voracious forces under which the city had relinquished all control. Other reports suggested the 17th Street Canal had been breached and some floodwaters were moving in our direction.

At about 6:30 AM the hurricane was at hand.

Slavery is well established in the Old Testament, and no doubt, well entrenched in New Testament scripture. Nonetheless, slavery and its stepchild, segregation, go against the enlightenment of humankind and of human nature and of course the nature of the universe.

-From a Runaway Slave

Day 2: Monday, August 29, 2005

2. The Storm Moves On

The sky was a clear pale blue on this blazingly hot Monday afternoon. The storm had rendezvoused at its next appointed destination. My cousin Pam came out on the balcony.

I said, "It looks good."

"I don't trust it," she said. "You can never know about these things. Storms are very tricky, you know. You have to watch out for what comes after them."

"It is over," I said. "I would like to get going before dark if all goes well. I don't want to take up any more of your guys' space and time than I have to. You have been quite kind to let me stay. I do want to give you some money as I promised." I went in and sat on the sofa bed. She talked to some passers-by, hesitated at the entryway, looked at me, and came inside.

PAM

For a long time family people have been talking about you. Mama said your old buddies Johnny and Jack warned you to leave. She never said why. I saw you once or twice when you came home on a trip from Chicago, then Los Angeles. I never got a chance to talk to you. Mama said you were her favorite nephew. You spent a lot of time at our house. Y'all talked a long time. I wanted to tell you about my job with the government. I have been there all these years.

Mama said you were the first one in the family to finish college. One day I came to your mother's house to see Mama. As I walked through the kitchen I heard them laughing in happiness that you had made the grade and crying in sorrow that you had to leave. Some years later I went to visit Mama when she was on her deathbed. Your mother had moved her into your old room. Mama had your graduation picture on her nightstand. As we talked her conversation soon got around to you.

"Mama, won't you please tell me why did he have to leave?" I asked. Mama paused and slowly glanced around the room. She closed her eyes for a moment as if to be searching inside herself for just the right words to tell me what I came to hear. With her hands in a prayer position, her eyes open slightly, she began to utter in a very low, slow voice:

"Early one Sunday morning just after the break of day we were on our way to worship in the house of God as we got closer to crossing the Tupelo Canal we heard them *screaming and hollering, 'They killed my boy! They have killed my little Henry!' His mom and dad with a few family members found his body in the Tupelo Canal. Them low down dirty peckerwoods killed him- everybody knows that. How low down can you get? They cut off his manhood and stuck it in his mouth. Someday they got to face judgment. They got to come face to face with their Almighty Maker. That's when the wrath of God will come down on them. That's when we will see justice done. You can mark my word on that."*

Mama continued. "White folks have always been the law down here you know, and they still are. In those days it didn't take much for an uppity Negro to cross them. We got along just fine as long as white folks were right. I don't know if that boy had crossed the line or not. Even if he did, still they had no right to kill him. Black people ain't never gonna get no justice on this earth."

Pam's story made me remember when Pam's mother, my Aunt Marion, called me one day and during our conversation she mentioned, "It would be nice to see you again." She did not say anything about being sick and nothing about a prolonged illness. My mother told me some years later that it was a deathbed request Marion had made, and she spoke about me just before she died. You know, I could have made the trip. My denial has plagued me to this day.

"Cousin, why won't you tell me the truth about why you left New Orleans as a young man? I don't understand," Pam said.

Someone knocked on the door. She said, "Come in." It was Bruce, the soldier from the apartment next door. The soldier wanted to bring us up to date on what was going on. The hurricane was over. All of the infrastructure was in very good shape. The real damage was at the 17th Street Canal. It was leaking, he said. He would keep us posted until his batteries gave out.

Pam and I went downstairs. The sun had set, nightfall was upon us. The water had seeped to the bottom of the tires. My cousin said, "It is rising, you see, you can't leave right now, you better stay the night."

"Ok, I will stay the night."

Before midnight on Monday the water had reached the bottom rung of the window.

Some of us were out in the heat of the mid-day sun down at the other end of the cotton field. The master was making his usual daily noontime check at our cotton patch. We gathered to hear his words about our work. There was talk, we said to the master, the word was all around that Mr. Lincoln had given us our freedom. "Master, why hasn't freedom come our way?"

The master took his good time, looked at each of us for a moment with unrepenting eyes, and in a firm, sound voice, in this unforgiving heat, said, "You are bonded to the land," as he faded away in the cotton patch. We all knew the master believed we could never be free.

-*From the Slave Journal*

Day 3: Tuesday, August 30, 2005

DAY OF NO RETURN

3. Leaving

4. The Parking Lot: Our Home

5. One Little Girl

6. Faded Dreams

7. Miss Agness

III

Leaving

Early Tuesday morning the cars were completely covered, the windows were floating around inside the car. I told my cousin that she was right – going home was now out of the question.

We heard female voices screaming for help. As we ran up to the balcony we saw four young ladies fending off snakes and an alligator in the water. Four young men and an older man from an apartment had jumped into the water with sticks, guns, and saved the ladies from any harm.

There was too much traffic in and out of the apartment. Pam and her daughter must have known everyone in the complex. About noon on Tuesday, a small police boat pulled up to the front of the apartment and an officer asked if he could speak to the occupants of our floor. We summoned everyone. The captain properly identified himself and introduced the other two officers under his command. The captain said his mission was to get us to safety if we wanted to leave. He said after he discharged this group of people, the crew would return at 2:00 PM for a pickup and his last trip would be at 4:00 PM, and if we did not take advantage of the offer we would be stuck here on our own. "There will be no other way out of here. Ok, see you guys at 2:00 PM." They pulled out.

We talked about leaving. The soldier said he and his girlfriend were staying. The man and woman from down the hall were in doubt about leaving. He decided he would stay. She said, "Ok." Pam could not make up her mind. She was worried about leaving her apartment. Her daughter had little choice in the matter. She would do whatever her mother said.

"I am leaving." I started packing and suggested they do the same. I wanted to be ready at 2:00 PM. Cousin said if we were not ready at 2:00 PM there was another boat at 4:00 PM, we could be packed by then.

The boat pulled up on time, and the officer said we could only take two suitcases per person. "I am ready," I said. Pam threw a small tantrum. She wanted to take all ten bags. She tried to explain to the captain she could not afford to leave her family valuables in such an unsafe apartment. Captain Johnson said, "Two bags or you don't go." She and her daughter got in the boat with two bags each.

The boat slowly backed out into the deep water, carefully avoiding our cars and other debris. As the boat accelerated I took one last long, heart-wrenching look at my car, which still had California plates, and had been a part of my life for such a long time. Now that was gone.

On our way, people on their balconies waved as we drove by. We picked up several people in the water who were just trying to make their way to dry land. We saw people on an overpass. Some were waving, shouting, others were coming and going, it appeared, with no place to go. We could not help them. Our boat was overloaded with people and did not stop.

Soon we arrived at the high grounds at the west end of a dead end street with no name. There were between seventy-five and a hundred people on this lot. After we were told to get out, we asked the officers where we were. Officer Johnson said, "Talk to the people in charge here." Some people were voicing their frustrations as we arrived. We joined them.

The officer joined the authorities already on the ground, exchanged amenities, returned to his boat, and drove away.

We asked the authorities, "Where are we?" and to give us some ideas of any plans they had for our departure.

Mr. Nichelson said to all of us, "Hopefully before the end of the day there will be some movement to take all of you out of here. We are waiting," he said, "on the boat to make its last trip back shortly after 4:00 PM."

Several boats arrived loaded with people, including the lady from down the hall. She was greeted with joy by my cousin. The officer in our boat told us they had been recalled to their home stations. We thanked him and his crew. He wished us well on our journey. After a few handshakes they departed.

The group had increased to about less than two hundred people. The officer in charge said he would like to get us out of there before the sun went down. It was now almost 5:00 PM, he said.

The lady from down the hall said she wanted to leave the apartment because the water had almost reached the balcony of the second floor. She said she was afraid to stay there over night with the place flooding the way it was.

In the evening several large flatbed trucks pulled in. The officer in charge, a Mr. Maxwell, said, "This is your transportation out of here." The drivers and the officers talked for some time before the driver and his crew came to address us. We wanted to know when we were leaving and where they were taking us. Mr. Maxwell would not tell us exactly, except he said, "Just a few miles from here."

The lead driver changed the conversation. He asked, "Where are you people from?" There were different responses. Most of the people answered from the 8th and 9th wards. "From the Lower 9th Ward," I told him. As he moved away from the others and back to his truck he beckoned me over. He said, "My family used to live back of Tennessee and Miro. Boy, my folks were spread all over back of town. All of that's long gone by now- you heard about the water coming in. Everything is flooded down there, man, everything is gone," he said. "My name is Willie, Reverend Willie Williams. I was the assistant pastor at Water Land Baptist Church."

"I grew up on Urquhart and Flood, went to McCarty Grammar School. I used to work at the station at St. Claude and Alabo after school. I am a McFadden, my name is Smitty." We shook hands.

Reverend Williams said, "My cousin Norman used to hang at that station all the time. You must be the guy he used to talk about. Y'all must have been good friends."

"Very good friends, good people," I said.

"Norman said that Smitty made it out of here a long time ago. He kind of indicated that, that Smitty had to go. He never said why. They said he wound up way out there in California. Norman been sick, bad sick for a long time. I don't see how he is going to come back. He will never pull through this. His health is too bad," Reverend Willie said.

"I would like to see him," I said.

"He is somewhere in Texas, maybe in Houston. We have family there. We pray for him all the time because we know he is not coming back."

"Where are you taking us?" I said.

"Down Main Street here about 10 or 12 blocks where the rest of the people are. As soon as I get the word from the officer in charge here we will get you people out of here today, to the next drop off point. If we can't get you all out of here today we will get you out of here tomorrow for sure. We will bypass the next drop off point and take you people directly to the Convention Center or to the Superdome. Man, let me tell you, I don't wish the Superdome on anybody. That place is a mess. They are robbing, shooting and killing people in that place."

Reverend Willie got his signal to move us out. We boarded the truck as he got into his cab and started the caravan. He made a left turn north onto Main Street. We were now on our way to the next drop off point.

IV

THE PARKING LOT: OUR HOME

As soon as we turned north the street had a slight upward grade, and you could see the properties on both sides had suffered very little damage if any. We were quite surprised.

We crossed an intersection and started to decline. It was obvious the hurricane had made its way through here. The damage was done. It was a sight- unbelievable. Nothing could have survived in its destructive path.

We traveled some distance and made a left turn and pulled into a huge lot west of the main street. The driver said, "This is home, folks."

We got out and looked around at the emptiness of the place with some degree of fright. There stood a dilapidated truck stop on the property which looked more like a bombed out bunker in some third world revolution.

We looked in and went inside. The floors of the entire building were covered with water. As we tip toed further in, the windows and doors were gone. The men and women's toilets had been ripped out. What was left were holes in the floor. Water was slowly running from a broken pipe in the ceiling. The challenge was just too great for some people. They did not know what to do.

A few of us walked to the curb to try to make some assessment of the place and what was going on. We noticed at the intersection about three blocks north of us there were so many people it was impossible to even estimate a count. Some people who had been down there said it looked like somewhere around three hundred to five hundred people just holding on.

At the truck stop our groups had swollen to somewhere around two hundred seventy-five to four hundred. The people were hot, angry, and showing signs of frustration. Yet there was no violence.

A large fire was ablaze in a fifty-gallon drum. They were cooking and eating. They were freely passing out all kinds of food. There were drums, guitar, one guy was beating sticks. We even saw one person playing a sax. People were dancing, talking, playing, and doing all sorts of things just trying to smother their anxieties. The people seemed to be doing it very well all by themselves. Children were playing all over the place and getting along well. There was a general feeling that the governmental authorities were not that concerned about us if at all. Some people thought we were on our own from the beginning.

Several groups were being formed- some were already together. I was asked to join with some people. I said, "It looks as if my cousins are forming a group. I will be with them." As I approached her group she walked over to me and I said, "How is it going?"

Pam said, "Let me finish this conversation. I will bring you up to date on everything tomorrow morning." She said, "Let me get back over here and finish up things with these people."

I said, "Who are these people? Do you know them?"

She said, "Yes. A lot of them are people I used to work and hang out with. They are from across the river. We may wind up over there when all this is over. See you in the morning," she said, turned and went back to her group.

I felt a little pushed away. I thought, "So what?" and went back to the other people.

V

ONE LITTLE GIRL

The sun had faded away. There were no street lights or lights of any kind. The flames of fire had dimmed to a glow. We were now consigned to the darkness. The games were over, the children seeking their parents for comfort.

I was talking to Howard about our conditions when his little girl, Amy, came over to him and said, "Daddy, I want to go home."

He hugged his child and mumbled, "Sure."

Again, she said, "Daddy why can't we go home? I am sleepy."

Two ladies, Mrs. Stella and Jenny, who were watching several of the children, came over and said to the father, "Let her come over and stay with the other children until your wife gets back. Your daddy can keep an eye on all of us."

He said, "Thank you." He turned to her with water in his eyes and said, "How can I tell my little girl we don't have a home to go to?"

She said, "You can't, don't even try. Tell her we are on our way home now- it just going to take us a little longer time to get there that's all."

"My wife and some other ladies are over there helping those older ladies who are sick. You know, they just didn't give us any kind of medical help. Look at this," he said. "Where is the help? They don't give a shit about us. They never did," he said.

"Yep. You got that right," Stella said. The father walked toward the sidewalk as he moved somewhat out of sight.

VI

FADED DREAMS

By this time I was beginning to feel the need for some shut-eye. It would be nice if I could get some. There was a slight fall in the temperature, but boy it was still hot as hell outdoors. I took a blanket out of my bag just in case it was needed. The bag was my pillow. I could smell the stench of the slow moving summer night breeze. In the distance you could hear the drum beats in competition with loud, sporadic, rapid gunfire. The helicopters which kept surveillance on us during the day were now long gone.

As the stars promenaded on their nightly journey across the sky I tried to find my connection with humankind. I did, however, locate Deneb, Vega and Altair, my favorite stars in the Summer Triangle, as I did so many years ago...

I remember the three of us were young boys, sitting on the side of the canal playing and talking. The Claiborne canal ran under the street at Caffin and trickled down to just a small stream at Lamanche. McCarty School was edged in the bank of the canal where so many students played during lunchtime. Alex, Joseph and I often played in the water.

One day, Miss Annie came by. We never knew what her real name was- everybody just called her Miss Annie. She was a little too dressy for a woman her age and always a bit on the sassy side. That was our Miss Annie.

She said, "Boys stop playing around. Let me tell you something. You boys got to stick together if we ever gonna change things down here. And I mean stick together. You boys can't tell things ain't right, right now. When you get grown you'll see what these white folks have done to us. They gonna keep their feet on our necks until we rise up and stop them. You see they want to keep us down forever, and I mean forever. Somebody got to stop them.

"Let me tell you another thing before I go- I am running a little late but let me say this and I am on my way. Take this with you throughout life and you boys will do well. Children, you got to know the difference between a stumbling block and a stepping stone. They are gonna throw so many stumbling blocks in our path just to defeat you. These white folks have never treated us right and they are trying to forget that. But you must never ever let them forget what they did to us.

"Now children will you please help Miss Annie get across this stumbling block? I can't go meet that handsome young principal with mud on my pretty brand new shoes. Now can I?"

After so many years of living outside of the South, I finally made my way back to New Orleans with deep mixed feelings. Yet, in spite of those feelings I went looking to connect with several old grammar school buddies. Before she got the door completely opened, Mrs. Sue, Alex's mother, said, "Son, you are back after all these years."

"Yes, Ma'am."

"I hope you are back on this side where you belong," she said.

"Yes Ma'am, I am."

"You know those people out there in Holy Cross are just like those white folks down there in St. Bernard. They don't give a damn about us," she said.

"It must have changed some over the years."

"Yes, it has, from white people to colored people. That's just about all, son," she said.

"How is Alex? If he is around I would like to talk with him a little bit, we had such great times when we were kids, you know."

"Alex found a career in the military. You know he became an officer and everyone around here was very pleased with what he had done. He was killed in a strange accident while on duty. The government never gave us the straight story of what really happened. We don't know what went wrong. I guess we'll never know." Sadly, Ms. Sue said, "You know he was our only son. He and Joyce from up the street got married and raised a family here. You should go see Joyce, you remember her? She lives a couple doors up from us. She would be glad to see you."

"So he married little Joyce after all? I didn't know that. Yes, I will see her. I heard he had a son?"

"Yes she did. At the tender age of nineteen, Albert was gunned down by some of them dopes. But the Lord be my witness I know deep in my heart that child, my only grandson, was not one of them dopees. It's been a long time. You gonna be okay?"

"Yes, I am gonna be alright."

"Me and the husband, we talk about you a lot you know. Anyway glad to have you back. God bless you son."

"Thank you ma'am."

Joseph's sister Betty told me that my other childhood buddy matured into a good father and raised a wonderful family. The community was proud of what the family had accomplished socially and politically. Joseph was devastated, she said, when it was learned that Mark, his only son, was indicted for bribery in just about the worst political scandal to hit this city.

We were naïve. Three young Black boys with big dreams and great hopes. They went in search of the promise, the two of them here in New Orleans. That freedom could be had by everyone in this Metropolis of the South. I brought my burning desire elsewhere in pursuit of the promise. We three young Black men discovered that the freedom we were in search of was never intended for those of our birth.

VII

Miss Agness

I laid back, tucked my bag under my head, secured the backpack between my legs for safety, and pulled the blanket up for cover. It had gotten a bit chilly. An older lady on her way by stopped. "Son," she said. "Are you asleep?"

"No ma'am," I said, and raised up.

"My name is Miss Agness. Your cousin, you were talking to her earlier tonight. That lady who lives down the hall from her- her name is Merelyn. All of them over there know each other for a long time now. When you were talking to some people your cousins got that group together. They hatched a plan and you are not included in it. You better figure out what you gonna do. Mister, keep your eyes open, that's all I gotta tell you. Take care of yourself."

"Thank you very much," I said, as she walked away.

I dozed for a moment or two. There was so much noise and too many people on the move. Yet I caught a few catnaps here and there.

Empire stands on murder.

Murder stands on profits.

Profits stand on slavery.

Slavery stands on the production of more slaves.

-From the Slave Journal

Day 4: Wednesday, August 31, 2005

DAY OF THE POLICE

VIII

ALL ABOUT THE FOOD

It was just about daybreak and you could tell it was going to be a scorcher even though the sun was not yet up. A couple guys came over in haste. James said in a commanding voice, "Smitty are you awake?"

"Yes, what's up?"

"We got some things we got to get straight."

"What things?"

"We got to straighten this bathroom shit out first thing. All these women will be up any minute, man. We can't have them bending over holes in the ground. That's alright for us men, but not for these ladies and girls."

Harry said, "There are all kinds of boxes and crates in the back. We can fix some of those and they can use as toilet seats." He brought a couple to show us.

Billy came over to me and said quietly, "You didn't know what the hell to do, did you?"

"Nope," I said. He giggled, and walked away.

"We got to deal with the food thing you know," Harry said. "These kids gonna be getting up any minute and they gonna want some food."

"Didn't they bring some food from home? Do we have any leftovers from last night?" I asked.

"All that's just about gone. Yeah, we got some left, but that won't be enough to feed the people. More people are joining the group. Everyone is talking about the food thing. What are we going to do about it?" Harry wanted to know.

About ten or twelve came over and Ben said, "Hey people, there is a way we can get over this food thing, man. We gotta go get these people some food, right?"

"Yeah," said Harry.

"Okay," Ben said. "There is a super-supermarket down the road about a mile and something over there."

"We know where that is," a couple people said.

"We just go in," Ben said, "get what we want, get back here, feed the people, it's all over, man."

Keith asked, "You mean, break in and just take these people's food?"

From voices in the group came, "That's stealing!"

Another said, "That store is just sitting there. If we don't go in someone else will and take what they want."

Ben said, "Look people. You know there is that big group a couple blocks up the street. They are about two times our size. If they beat us to that store, man, we are shit out of luck. Our best bet is to get our shit together, get down to the damn store, get in any way we can, do whatever, get the hell out, come back here and feed these people. What's the big fricken deal?"

Among the men, tempers were heating up. The ladies were quiet, yet seemed uneasy about what was going on. Linda said in a hesitant voice, "Our problem is you men can't ever seem to get your act together."

Another lady, Marg, echoed, "You can bet that's our problem all right."

In the mix of all of this several people came over. An older fellow, Horace, said, "Mr. Smitty, you have been pretty quiet over here. What do you think we ought to do?"

Harry said, "What is your take on all this?"

Before I could say anything Linda said, "Goddamn I don't give a shit what Mr. Smitty's take is. I have three children that's gotta be fed when they get up."

Her friend Gail said, "I got two little ones who wants to eat as soon as they get up."

"Let him speak," Harry said. "We need to let him say what he has to say."

"Thank you. Now listen," I said. "I don't like the idea of breaking into somebody's store, taking, stealing what's not ours. That does not sit well with me. But our first job is to feed these women and children. We must be willing, if that time ever comes, to give account of ourselves. All of us. Here is my take on what I think we ought to do. Earlier on one lady said we can't seem to get our act together. On this issue all of us are together. Here is what I think: go in any way you can."

"We know how to get in," Ben said. Lots of laughs.

"We are taking food. Watch the stuff that will spoil in this hot weather. Be very careful of the meats- they have been in there a couple of days without refrigeration. We don't want anybody getting sick, you know. Take all of the water and toilet paper you can carry. We can use them in the next days if we can't get any more or get out of here. Get all the can goods and stuff like cereal you can. Now guys, no contraband or any kind of weapons, alcohol, cigarettes, and any of that kind of stuff."

"You mean we can't even take a few brews and some smokes?" Ben said.

"That's right. Ladies, don't let these guys come back without water and toilet paper, and ladies don't forget to take care of your needs."

"Well, let's wish them well Mister Smitty," said Linda as she came over. "I apologize for the way I talked to you earlier today. Please forgive me, I am sorry."

"Thank you for coming over. I accept your apology," I said.

IX

THE POLICE STANDOFF

It was a bright, hot morning even though the sun was not quite overhead. A few of the people from the group up the street were passing but didn't offer any information.

As we looked up the streets for a few minutes we caught a glimpse of our group running toward us as fast as they could. They were yelling, "Come help us carry some of this shit!" We did.

"Man," Ben said, "you don't know what the hell we have been through."

BEN

When we got there the place was loaded with cops. They had the whole place surrounded. All the windows and doors were broken out. The place was all taped off with that yellow and black tape shit. When we first came up we thought the cops were guarding the place. As we got closer, man, those bastards were getting over big time. They told us, "Get the hell away from round here." We checked out their vehicles. Man they had them big 54 inchers, bikes, radios, and all the electronic shit you can think of! They had guns, cigarettes, booze that would last them for months. They had computers and all that shit. That one cop who was screaming at us had a toilet and a toilet seat tied on top that big ass SUV as if he was gonna take a crap on the road.

We told the cops again, "We got children we got to feed."

One cop said, "I am telling you people once and for all you can't go in there. This is a police matter."

"With all that crap you got stashed in your trucks you say this is a police matter?!"

One cop said, "Here comes the captain. Let him handle this." After talking to his men the captain walked over to us.

Harry said, "We have children to feed and we have seniors who need food."

"You people want to break the law you can be arrested on all sorts of charges."

Linda said, "We have children to feed who have not eaten since yesterday. Captain, I don't give a damn about your charges. We are not leaving here without food."

"So if you want to arrest somebody you better start now," One of our guys shouted. "We have five hundred hungry people over there."

In a light voice the captain told his men, "Make sure they don't take anything other than food. They are our cover, you know what I mean. Let them in." The captain loaded up his car and drove off.

We went in, got some brews, we couldn't pass up the cigarettes so we copped a few cartons, not many. We got some wine and some other goodies, but none of the hard stuff. The cops were on our case every time we made a move. They wouldn't let us get anywhere near the warehouse where the real booze was stashed.

My man here and Jack, that guy over there, got in the back door, snatched some cases of the hard stuff. We got the hell out in a hurry.

"When they figure out it was us who went in, they are gonna be P.O.'d," Ben said. "We gotta hurry up and find a place to stash the stuff. The cops may show up any minute. I don't trust them bastards."

Billy said, "After everybody get some eats we gonna bust out some of that cold brew- in this weather that gonna be good. What are we gonna do if some of those people from up the streets want some of our food?"

"We gonna give them some," said Ben.

"Yeah, man, we got plenty," Harry said. "We are gonna share some, you know."

Billy said, "We ought to wait till later on after the sun goes down when the real party starts to bust out the good stuff."

Harry said, "Man, let me tell you one thing. Later on ain't promised to none of us. Man, we may as well get it on as we got it on and let later on take care of itself."

"I heard that," Ben said.

The last of the morning dew had evaporated under the midday sun. Everyone seemed to have gotten enough food. There was plenty of water and toilet paper. The boys and girls were tasting the brews and playing a little music. The kids were playing, dancing, and the older people were in a nice mood.

X

THE POLICE COMMANDER

Ken, one of the people who had been checking out safe places to stash the goods, said, "If we go down the street about two blocks and turn left there are lots of flooded out houses where we can stash our goods. Everything looks good over there," he said. "But we still need bodies to hang with the stuff just in case something goes wrong. They can get back over here in a breeze. Come on everybody, let's get these goodies moving before them cops figure it was us who got them for the goods," he said.

Harry said, "If them boys were that damn smart they wouldn't be cops anyway."

Lots of people said, "You got that right."

"Like I said before, when the cops figure this thing out they will be over here in nothing flat. We gotta get this stuff out of here. This place gotta be cleaned up. We can't have anything around here that looks like it came from that market. Let's get it done folks," Ken said.

Several loads had been moved to the hideout when two police cars and three SUVs pulled up, stopped, gave us a good going over, took some notes without getting out of their vehicles, and slowly drove up the street. They stopped at that large crowd of people about three blocks north of us. As far as we could tell they walked through the crowd and pulled some people aside. We could not tell what was going on. Horace told our people, "Don't go anywhere near that police action. It could get bad for us. We don't need any more problems than we already have. The police were up there about thirty minutes, got in their cars, turned left, and drove west into the city.

Ken said, "These cops passing us like that don't smell like ok to me. Let's hurry up and move this stuff out of sight. I can't see them boys not coming back, not after that once over they gave all of us." After awhile the moving was done. Everyone seemed to have taken part in the clean up. The place was clean. Some of the smell was gone and we felt good.

The grass was hot and dry. The kids were running around. The old heads were feeling good. The mood was nice. About twenty-five people walked by our group. Alvin said, "We have some smokes. You folks are welcome to partake in the goodies if you are of a mind to."

Some of our group said, "Okay, why not," and joined the movement.

Alvin looked at the rest of us and said, "A little indulgence in the good stuff in these harsh and bitter days will certainly help ease the pain." As they walked away he said, "We gonna hold up in that old flooded building about a block down the road on the other side of the street. If any of you brothers or sisters have a change of heart come and get with us."

"Thank you, but we better stand pat. Somebody gotta keep an eye on what's going on," Ken said.

Some of us walked up the street seeking shelter from the blistering heat of the sun. We found some shade under these once majestic pink magnolias, which were leaning up against each other as they had been uprooted by the unforgiving storm with impunity. We talked a bit about our best option- the Superdome, the Convention Center, or the streets. Everyone rejected the Superdome. It was the Convention Center or the streets.

Before anything got settled some people from our larger group began pointing and shouting lightly so as not to be heard or seen by the oncoming cars. There were no sirens blasting, none of the lights were on. The vehicles had a slow but persistent movement in our direction. They stopped in front of our large parking lot where they could see and speak to everyone. There were three police cars and five police SUVs. The evacuees had little or no way out. Some of our people said, "We better get back down the street- it looks like things might get shitty."

The police exited the vehicles and their leader with a bullhorn summoned everyone to the curb. It was unusual to see a commander directing this kind of operation. A few people went to the sidewalk, others stayed put. The commander moved to the edge of the field and announced, "This is a police matter and everyone is under my orders. I want everyone who took part in the break-in this morning at the supermarket to come forward. These policemen are here to retrieve all the stolen properties and we will not leave until all of the properties are in our possession. The people who are responsible will be taken into custody. If we don't get all of the goods back immediately I am authorized to arrest everyone in this lot, and I mean everyone."

Horace said, "Looks like we are already under arrest." As we got closer to the center of things the commander was in a face-to-face encounter with this elderly lady whom some of us knew. She was doing all the talking and pointing her finger at the commander and in every direction. It looked like they knew each other.

The years had added some middle weight to her once petite, fragile frame. She had high cheekbones with deep red skin, long, cold black hair, yet it was difficult to tell she was not of full blood. She said her tribe, like many others, stole away, drifted south during the forced migration from the delta to the Oklahoma territory. Some said she was Chickasaw. She said, "I am Choctaw, most will never know, but one thing we all know Miss Vera is always on fire." She said, "I am a longtime resident of the Lower 9th Ward. Our family lived back of town on the Florida swamp. With what little things we could carry we finally made our way to St. Claude to get the help we had been promised, yet no help was in sight. Commander," she said, "we have been struggling back there all our lives just to keep a roof over our heads and a little food in our bellies. Now you want to put us all in jail? You go right ahead Mr. Commander. Take us all away," the old lady said.

The officer said, "I am here to enforce the law and get the stolen property back."

She said, "What damn property?" She looked around as she was talking and saw our group. "Smitty, is that you?"

I said, "Yes."

She said, "Get your butt over here. Do you know who this man is?"

"No."

"He is one of them Brussets from out front of town," she said. "You mean to tell me you don't remember them?"

"I remember the Brussets. I went to McCarty with some of those folks from across St. Claude, but I don't remember him."

"Well," she said, "whether you remember him or not, he is our commander who used to live in that forsaken Holy Cross neighborhood." You could feel the power in his handshake. The commander was a man beyond six feet with a posture of a palace guard and spoke with as much authority. He had a full head of light brown hair mingled with gray. The commander had a bright olive complexion tanned by the sun as age had slightly begun to evidence itself. Yet the years had preserved his manliness. His manner was every bit consistent with that of an officer who represented his profession only too well. The commander said, "I take it most of you are from across the Canal on the back of town side of Holy Cross?"

Miss Vera said, "We are from the Lower 9th Ward and proud of it."

We heard the words of an old man standing away from the group with an almost piercing voice where everyone could hear. "My name is Eddie Terrell. Miss Vera is right, Commander. When they built that canal, the 9th ward was broken up forever. The whole place from the canal to Jackson Barracks and from the river to the swamp is the Lower 9th Ward," he said. "You all broke up the

Lower 9 when you created that ever forsaken Holy Cross district. Anything north of St. Claude, the dividing line, as you want to call it, was cut out as if we did not exist."

Miss Vera said, "Commander, don't you stand here and try to deny what you all did to us. With all the privileges you all had, you folks never tried to help us out, not once that I can remember."

Mr. Eddie said, "I agree with Miss Vera. She is a friend and a longtime resident of the Lower 9."

The officer paused for a moment as if her words had touched him in some kind of way. "Miss Vera," he said, "your age and all that you have suffered have earned you my utmost respect, if nothing more. Let me say this to all of you folks who don't know the place. Miss Vera and Mr. Eddie know my family roots go back to the beginning of time in this community. My father was the Inspector General at the Port. He received a good education, worked very hard all his life, and earned that position which he kept until his retirement. He passed a few years ago. Mr. Eddie, you must have known him."

Mr. Eddie said, "I did and I am sorry for your loss."

The commander said, "Miss Vera knew my dad from long years ago."

Ms. Vera responded, "Without a doubt, Commander, and I am sorry for your loss."

The commander continued.

COMMANDER BRUSSET

We were always criticized by the people north of St. Claude for having an easier and better life than most of you people. And for not helping you folks out at all. In some instances that may well have been the case. I don't live in Holy Cross anymore but what I am about to say may be of some comfort to you as it was to us. My father said to the family, "We must do what we have to do to get ahead." We kept our families together, stayed out of trouble and our education was equal to or better than most whites. Our families were told we had to be twice as good as whites to get half of the goods they got. "Education," my dad said, "is the recipe for our success." What the north side really got upset about was that some of us got very good jobs and positions downtown and were able to move into all white neighborhoods. We left without reaching back and pulling up the people in the Lower 9.

Look people, we did not create this system. It was made long ago, not by us, nor was it made to our liking.

We found it the way it is just like you, so don't blame us for the problems. In those days we tried, like everybody else to use the system to our best advantage. Our families found ways like so many others, and we did what so many others did. We have no regrets. This city has always had a large number of people passing, everybody knows that. Look folks, it afforded us with a new and better way of life for us and our families. What you folks in the Lower 9 never realized was once you crossed over, the risk of going back for any reason was just too great. So why shouldn't we have aspired for a better life, since we were given all the gifts to attain our dreams for a better life for our families? If passing did it for us and so many others, so be it. Folks, there were two different worlds back when I came up. Mr. Eddie can tell you that. I don't know how much has changed since those days, if anything.

"Some things definitely have changed in your day, Sir," Mr. Eddie said. "If you lived north of St. Claude, that great dividing line, you would never be caught in that Holy Cross district unless you worked at the cotton warehouse or as some sort of domestic worker. If not you could be in police custody in nothing flat. But Commander, some things seemed to have changed so very little from your day with the Black ruling class in Holy Cross. It is their deeply

80

embedded, may I say, insidious Black on Black discrimination they hold against all of us in the Lower 9 who don't live in Holy Cross. They always wanted to keep this community segregated and that in and of itself has kept the Lower 9 from coming together," Mr. Eddie said.

Mr. Dabon said, "Hear me out people, and you too Commander. Folks, I went to join the Holy Cross Association. This white lady was very polite and said the Association would certainly appreciate my membership. The lady asked, 'Where do you live?'

"I said, 'Andry and Urquhart.'

"She said, 'Listen, you can join the association and come to all of our regular meetings and participate in many of our functions, Mr. Dabon. Sadly, you have to live in Holy Cross in order to vote and take part in the association's political process.' She said, 'St. Claude is our dividing line and I see you live two blocks north of the line.'

"I said, 'Lady, what are you talking about, this is taxation without representation in its crudest form!'

"'Mr. Dabon,' she said, 'We will assure you every effort will be made that you are well represented in the process even though you are unable to vote.'

"I withdrew my application and as I was leaving it occurred to me that these folks soon may have some sort of a restrictive covenant against those of us who live north of Holy Cross." Mr. Dabon said, "That's your old neighborhood, Commander. Do you think much has changed?"

The commander said, "I am here to carry out my orders as an officer of the law. The department does not pay me to engage in this kind of behavior. Nobody gave me or my family anything and that's what you people don't seem to understand. We don't owe anybody in the Lower 9th Ward nor anyplace else anything."

Mr. Dabon said, "Someone helped to set the stage for you and your family to open the doors to your success. The problem we had with you and your family, Sir, is that we never dreamed you would slam the doors in our faces. Commander, you and your family helped to keep us out." Mr. Dabon said, "Commander, you seem to be telling us these gifts you possess were bestowed upon you through some kind of divine intervention, yet we feel these very gifts may well have been an accident of history."

Before the officer could utter a word, Miss Vera stepped forward and got as close as she could, looked the officer dead in the face and said, "Mr. Brusset, my son. If you could just take a long, hard look back when the first ships breached the Mississippi, there upon was human cargo bound to its deck as stock and trade to the highest bidder in the new world. She offered little resistance in agony on her back in the cotton field as the master's son had his way. Those immoral and criminal acts, Commander," she said, "gave birth to the Brussets and others of your kind."

The commander knew the mood had changed as he perused this troubled crowd as any officer would. Without a sound he looked at Mr. Eddie with sympathy for a man of old age. Mr. Dabon was a much younger man and a bit more competitive. It appeared the officer did not want at this time a confrontation. He looked at Miss Vera for a few moments as if he was seeking redemption from a mother to her son. Still not a word. The commander took one step back, made a right turn, summoned his patrolmen and in a single formation they marched to their vehicles.

It was another burning day. We could feel the scorched earth under our feet as the police vehicles sped away with sirens blasting and lights flashing.

XI

KILLERS OF THE DOGS

There was a large empty lot adjacent and to the west of our lot. We saw a police car pull to the side of the street. The sergeant waved two trucks into the lot. Several people ran over to see what the heck was going on.

The driver opened the back doors and some twenty-five or so dogs jumped out. The lot was enclosed on three sides by a picket fence. The dogs ran around the lot and could have gotten away. The fence could not hold them back if they wanted to jump over it. The dogs slowly made their way back to the front and came face to face with their executioners. They seem to know they had been consigned to die. The executioners drew their weapons, aimed, and fired one shot in the head of each dog. All the dogs went to their death without a whisper except three dogs lay dying but not yet dead. Everyone was shouting, screaming, "Stop! Stop! Why are you killing these dogs?" We were all horrified.

The executioner in charge shouted, "Don't come any closer. Back up," he said. We did. "I have my orders. Don't interfere. This is police business."

Many people were shouting and screaming, "These dogs have rights, don't you know that? Those three aren't even dead. Why are you making them suffer so much, man? Why don't you finish the job? Just kill them!"

Joe said, "The bastards are making these poor animals suffer too much. How can the police do this? Who gave these orders?"

"In case you people don't know it, New Orleans is now under martial law," the sergeant said. "The police orders come down from the High Commander in Baton Rouge. We were ordered to round up all the stray dogs running the streets. These dogs will go mad in a couple days and attack humans. Don't you people know that? We don't have the facilities to put them asleep. We have to kill them where we find them. And people, it only takes one bullet to kill an animal and they can only use one bullet per dog." The executioner said, "You don't have to worry about those dogs. They will be dead soon enough." We could see these dying animals struggling to hold on to every breath of life as they lingered at the brink of death.

The other two executioners had already gone. We were still at a stand off with the sergeant. He repeated several times in a stringent voice, "I have my orders. Don't go near the animals." During the standoff, another truck was waved in. Two men got out who were not policemen.

One asked the executioner, "How many you got for us this time?"

The executioner said, "About the same as usual, twenty-five maybe thirty. But before you do anything make sure you check the wounded ones over there and see if any is still alive."

The man went over and he called back, "There is nothing over here but a bunch of dead dogs." The two drivers retrieved the dead animals, gave the high sign and drove away. Without a sound the executioner followed.

Most of the group were consumed in the animal slaughter and for a moment had forgotten about their personal devastation. We were returning to the groups and we noticed two young ladies seated on the ground in tears. They were overcome by the events. They were consoled and helped back to the groups. So many were in disbelief. Others were simply alarmed. Everyone was trying to grapple with these senseless killings as best they could. It probably would take some time before people could settle many of these emotional issues.

I found a little quiet spot behind a burned out trailer, which was not a bad place to do a bit of reflecting and maybe a doze or two. Anyway, I had to make a pit stop. After thinking about this for a moment I thought, *the killing of those dogs exemplified the arrogance of empire.*

That cherished power of empire exhibits its righteousness through the ruthless murder of innocent people and the unspeakable slaughter of helpless animals. Humankind, as we know, long ago instituted murder, and subsequent generations sanctified murder and made it holy. Our generation made murder for profit the new economic order of the empire. Whatever the outcome of all this, it may not be the kind of outcome we are hoping for.

XII

The Convention Center

It was a burning hot, humid summer day. The sun had reached the three quarter mark across the sky and was moving on. As we looked down the street we saw several eighteen-wheelers headed in our direction. They pulled to the curb, opened the back doors. We ran to the street to see what was going on. They were the kinds of refrigerated wheelers that carry slaughtered meats.

The supervisor using a bullhorn said, "We are here to pick you people up. This is your ride out of here."

Ben shouted, "You gonna put us in those refrigerated trucks, lock the doors, and drive away, that's it?"

The supervisor said, "Yes, we have to lock you people in. The doors must be locked. That's the way it is done. Rules, you know."

Ralph said, "You are not putting us in any locked trucks. Man, you want us to get in those locked trucks, and you won't even tell us where you are taking us! The only thing you said is 'Get in!' Man, that's bullshit. We ain't getting in. Look mister man, we just saw them kill a bunch of dogs over there for no reason. How do we know you are not gonna take us some place in those locked trucks and do us in for no reason?"

Horace said, "This brother is right. They have not given us anything, no food, no water, not telling where we are going. Now they are telling us to get in. This shit looks like it is by design. From what I am picking up on they have a plan set up just for us. They don't want that many of us back in the city. This shit has been mapped out for a long time- the *get rid of them* plan."

Reverend Willie noticed the group getting upset. He ran over to the supervisor and then to us. The reverend and I made the friendly exchange. We were on good terms. The reverend asked me what was going on. I said, "Why don't I let one of these other guys tell you what is going on."

Ben said, "Everybody here is pissed, angry, man, now the man came here with his bullhorn, not telling the people anything. He is gonna lock us in like we are a bunch of animals! All he wants us to do is say yes and get in. These people ain't gonna take any more of his shit. You better go back over there and tell that white SOB that." The reverend went over and talked to the supervisor and then told us they were going to see what they can do about the situation. The supervisor and all the wheelers drove away.

Since we were getting so little information about our neighborhoods, folks were beginning to focus on their individual problems. They wanted to hear about family, friends, and their houses. The big question that came up over and over was how long is it going to take them to get us back home. Some people said, "A couple days, by the weekend if not before."

Joann said, "Might go home tomorrow- things don't look that bad."

Jack said, "Why don't they let us stay here tonight and go home tomorrow? Why are they taking us to the Convention Center?"

Joann jumped in and said in a strong voice, "I don't want to go to the Superdome, the Convention Center, or any of that shit. I just want to go home." How little did we know.

Several large flatbed trucks with open tops and removable sides pulled in.

The reverend said, "Look at these trucks! We came back to take all of you folks out. I had to fight hard to keep you all out of the Superdome. Mr. Smitty," he said, "We are going to the Convention Center. How do you like that?"

I said happily in a loud voice, "The Convention Center!"

The people echoed, "The Convention Center!" No one wanted the dreaded Superdome.

The reverend made sure everyone was tucked in. Those flatbed trucks were way over crowded. It was going to be a slow and dangerous drive to the Center. The reverend gave the signal to the other drivers and we were finally on our way to a better place: The Convention Center.

The trucks were moving slowly through the streets. Our truck was in a good mood until we saw the crowds of displaced people on the streets of New Orleans. There were so many people begging for help yet there was so little we could do. We did, however, manage to share a little food, water, and some toilet paper. We saw young people muddling around doing nothing, others moving about going no place. As we looked into their faces, the children seemed lost, the elderly appeared resigned to defeat. "How long have you folks been on the streets?" we asked.

Some said, "A couple days."

Others said, "We don't know."

As we moved toward the Center the joy we once had rapidly faded away. So many people were overcome by sadness. Some were crying. Still others were quietly staring up into the skies. It was still in broad daylight and we had finally arrived at the threshold of our destination: the Convention Center.

We arrived across the street from the Convention Center. Yet it was about a block or so away. We were parked in a large lot and it looked like there were all kinds of instructions going on about the place. Reverend Willie and the crew told us, "This is your drop off point. You are home for now." There was a small wooden structure, which was probably used by the workers.

A worker said, "You can't go inside the building. They are going to take the building down first thing in the morning. You folks can stay outside and sleep here tonight. If anybody wants to go to the Convention Center you can take this side street- it runs directly into the Convention Center as you can see." As we looked around we could see the skylines of the business district unfold before our eyes. It appeared all was well. Some of us left the groups of people and surveyed the surrounding area.

The Convention Center was a whole other world. The place was in chaos. There were so many people it was unbelievable. Hordes of people moving around from one place to another with no place to go. By this time our groups were splitting up and going different places. Some even talked about going to the parking lot at the Superdome. We met up with some people who had been at different parking lots and had gone over to the Superdome. They told us of some of the horrible conditions inside the

Superdome itself. The outside of the Dome had so many people you could not get any kind of feeling of safety. The noise was loud inside- it was simply madness. They said, "You don't want to go to the Dome." At the Convention Center on this side of the street some homemade makeshift toilets were put up before we got there.

There were so many people already outside at the Center when we got there, and it looked like many of the flatbed people knew some of the people already there. Old groups were breaking up and new groups forming. Most of the people in our group were kind of at a loss. We did not know what to do. Our group had broken up except for about ten or fifteen people.

My cousin Pam seemed to know more than a few people. She brought over about twenty to twenty-five people. She asked, "What do we think the number of people should be?"

Kim said, "Looks like we have thirty-five to forty people and new ones coming in." We don't know the number we are going to wind up with. Maybe fifty. That may be too many for this place.

Billy said, "That number may have been alright when we were on the street. How are we going to fit all of us together in the Center?"

Ben said, "Let's go over and check this place out." About ten of us with my cousin went over and checked out the sleeping place. We would need a place large enough for fifty people or more. After about thirty minutes walking around the place we knew there was no chance we could get that many people together in one place.

Ben said, "Since we don't know the place maybe we should sleep outside tonight."

Billy said, "I am not sold on this place for tonight. Since we can see there will be so much movement in the place maybe we can find a good spot where we can protect each other." While we were talking a scuffle broke out in the Center. People started running, stumbling over each other everywhere. Some men rushed over and stopped the fight. The talk was it was a trivial matter, but it convinced us that the outside would be better for our protection, since we didn't know what went on there late at night.

Pam asked me, "What do you think?"

I said, "I am with the outside sleepers." We found a place directly across the street from the Center. We could hear and see most of the action at the Center and up and down the streets. We could see people coming and going. And if something big happened we had several get away exits. You bet the outside was our best bet.

"What we need to do," Harry said, "is form a circle, let the guys go find some folding chairs if possible. Place the chairs around the outside of the circle. If anyone tries to get inside the circle they will stumble over the chairs."

Kim said, "We will have to keep watch, we can't make fires over here like the other place."

Billy said, "We got water and we got toilet paper. One of us has got to stay with that stuff all of the time. Where are the toilets? Where do the people go?"

Billy said, "There is a long walkway around that wooden wall there and it breaks off into one side for the women and the other for the men."

I said, "Cousin, I want to take another look inside the Center and check the whole place out as much as I can before it gets dark. I don't want to be in that place after dark since I don't know anybody over there. In any event I will see you in the morning." The toilets were completely out of order. The smell of waste was everywhere. A couple of faucets had running water and the others were totally disconnected. There were a few safety lights here and there high in the ceiling. So many people stretched out all over the floor. You had to step over some to move around. Older people were up against the wall crying and weeping-you could feel their pain. The Center, as you moved around, was inexcusably dirty. Garbage was everywhere. I kept moving and looking, trying to avoid despair the like of which I had never witnessed before. There was not a public agency to be found. This country touts itself on being benevolent to those in need. What was going on here? In spite of the terrible conditions it came to me that this place was all we had and we must make the best of it.

XIII

THE LADY FROM ARABI

I was hoping to find a friendly face or two, but I was not sure about that. I kept moving and looking- the people's faces had merged into the darkness. Out of this dimness a voice said, "I know you, Smitty."

I said, "Yes," after recognizing the face and, "What are you folks doing here?"

Sandra said, "That's a story. Take a seat." There were about twenty-five or thirty in the group. Everyone was elderly except the Sandra and her mother. I looked at the people. They were completely out of their element. They were frightened and you could see the fear all over them. They appeared to be somewhat relieved to have me there and invited me to take a seat. The lady said, "We are all from the Parish- Arabi and Chalmette. My mother and I are hosting these elderly people to a residential home in Mississippi. We were scheduled to meet a chartered bus to take us there. We could not come straight to the hotel because we had to make so many detours- many of the streets flooded. It was hours later before we pulled up at the hotel. By that time the bus had long gone. The manager said we could stay the night at the hotel and he would try to contact the sheriff's department sometime today or tomorrow morning. The bad news came the next morning, that the hotel had to be evacuated by orders of the Fire Marshall.

"The manager said, 'The Superdome is closer- I wouldn't take anybody over there- you may not get out of there alive. Your best bet is the Convention Center. It's not a pretty place, but you and your group will probably be alright there.' He said he would personally make sure we got over here safely. Mother thanked him for his hospitality and here we are."

"Where do you know him from?" an older man asked, referring to me.

"He used to come into the store," Sandra answered.

"Did he hang around long?" he asked.

"No," she said. "He would come in and buy books and things. We would talk a little bit like I did with everybody else."

A lady asked, "You didn't live in Arabi did you? And if you didn't live in Arabi where did you live?"

Sandra said, "He did not live in Arabi. He lived in New Orleans."

The old man jumped in and said, "There used to be a whole slew of coloreds on the other side of Perez."

The old lady said, "I thought there were a few on our side too."

"To the best that I know," the old man said, "There were a few Negroes working on our houses and taking care of our children, that's about all. They were not living in our neighborhood."

Another lady said, "I don't know for sure but my guess is that most of the Blacks lived in Chalmette."

Another man said, "Years ago there used to be a whole bunch of coloreds on that street between the cemetery and the monument. All the whites down here can tell you after the War Between the States the northerners built that place for the Negroes. The land ran from St. Bernard Highway clear back to the Mississippi River. That land has always belonged to the whites."

Sandra said, "I never heard of the place."

Her mother said, "It was called Fazendeville. The street sign is still there."

"What happened to all those people who used to live there?" Sandra asked.

Her mother said, "I really don't know. They just moved away I guess."

The old man said, "The government wanted to expand the cemetery but did not have the money to pay for it. The people of St. Bernard wound up, as always, paying the cost of buying the coloreds out. We paid the coloreds way too much for the property. By right that property belongs to us. We didn't owe them one brown copper cent for that property. When the northerners came down and freed them from the land and told them they were free to go that did not free them from the debt they owed their owners. There was no sunset to the debt. The debt followed them to the grave. What could we do to get them out? We had no choice but to pay them too much as we have always done."

"Look folks," I said. "You can bet your life I am not from the Parish. I live in the Lower 9th Ward. I can't speak for everyone in my neighborhood. But like many Black people who know the misdeeds of the Parish, the hatred runs too deep."

My friend stepped in and said, "Smitty, don't get into an argument with these people. It's not worth it."

I said, "Folks, I want to thank you for having me."
Some said, "Thanks for stopping by."

"It is getting late."

Sandra said, "Let's connect tomorrow."

"Tomorrow." I moved on.

Why didn't they give us some land so we could have a state outright? They knew that would be equality. No way, man, that would be too much like right. Our own state. When has the Man ever done right by us? These folks would never let that righteous stuff go down.

Look, the White Man wants us down, alright? All the way down where he would not have to raise his foot too high to put it on our necks to keep us down right here in this Land of the Free.

-Big Mack talking at the Convention Center; 2005

Day 5: Thursday, September 1, 2005

CHILDREN OF THE STORM

14. Farewell Cousins

15. Fazendeville

16. Sister, Sister

17. The Army Runs Out of Food

18. Kids and Segregation

19. False Alarm

20. The Watchful Eye

XIV

FAREWELL COUSINS

The sun hadn't pierced the atmosphere on this early Thursday morning yet the Center was engulfed in a burning, blistering heat.

I was in the process of getting some sort of schedule for the day. I didn't want to spend my time just hanging around waiting for something to happen. I was desperate to get something done. I could not sleep anyway. The first light had already broken. My cousin showed up with a gang of fifty or more friends. "Who are these people and where did they all come from?" I asked.

She said, "These are my friends. I have known all of them for quite some time."

I said jokingly, "They all are a pretty dizzy-looking bunch- worse than the first group of your friends I met. But they are your friends- that's all that matters."

"We all are trying to get to Houston. My daughter and I are trying to get to Chicago where my government job is still open. I need to get to Chicago before the end of the month or at least notify them of my intentions," Pam said.

"How are you and your daughter and the rest of this mob going to get to Houston from where you are now standing?"

She said, "Look. The first thing we need to do is get to the Airline Highway 61 just above Carrollton where the army helicopters are taking people to the airport. We are going to walk from here to the Airline Highway. If the 10 Freeway is opened we will use that to get to the 61. If the freeway is closed then we will have to use the streets."

The people who came from the Superdome said, "Don't even think of going through Jefferson Parish to get to the airport. You will never make it. They are turning Black people back at the Jefferson Parish line."

"Since we don't know what the government is going to do we have to do something for ourselves," Pam said. "Well Smitty, what are your plans for getting out of here?"

I said, "I got no plans for getting out of here. Here is what I think. Nagin has just about disbanded the police force. They are like a bunch of vigilantes enforcing their own rule of law up and down the streets. On the other side you have the army and the National Guard with their fingers on the triggers of their guns and, oh yes, you have these idiot bad guys who are so darn crazy they are shooting up each other. We hear the gunfire every night. And now you want me to walk forty or fifty blocks to some helicopter pick-up point that may or may not exist? No way. Cousin, you know I don't have a plan. But here is a bit of my thinking off the top of my head. The longer we stay here, the more people, more refugees they bring here, the better are our chances of getting out of here. We got some news, by word of mouth grant you, that Nagin said there are about ten thousand to twenty thousand people at the Convention Center without food, water, or toilet paper. That condition to me demands their immediate attention. This large number of desperate, hungry refugees works in our favor. Neither the government nor the city wants that many refugees becoming violent. It would be another national disgrace. They don't want another disgrace on their hands. I am not leaving. That's my take on the matter."

Pam said, "It is time for me and our group to be on our way before the heat gets hotter, as it will. We were glad to have you with us for these few days. I am your first cousin, you know. I want to give you a hug and a promise that some day you will tell me some of the things you hold deep inside of you." She said, "Will you make that promise?"

I said, "Dear cousin, the answers you are seeking, please understand, were long ago laid to rest in another world we cannot invade. It was very nice to be with you all this time. After all, we are cousins. As the old folks would say, blood runs deeper than water, but not that deep." Yet as we parted we both seemed to feel somewhat itchy. For sometimes my cousin never included me in the conversations with her friends from Algiers or elsewhere. It would have been ok if she had just said, "These are my personal friends and our conversations are private." Today it became clear that I was not to be included in the Houston trip. I wished them well and I also had to move on.

XV

Fazendeville

I wanted to see Sandra from Arabi before she left. I wanted to talk to her a little bit about what the Parish was all about. It looked like they were not there. Henry said, "They are gone, if you are looking for those people you were talking to yesterday."

"Yes," I said.

Henry said, "They left real early this morning- 6:00, 6:30 or so. The sheriffs came by and picked them up. Me and my man here helped them put their bags and all the other things in the three vans the sheriffs came in. She seemed like a nice lady and she gave us a little folding money for what we did."

Larry said, "They sure got them out of here in a hurry. They got here yesterday and gone today."

"Gone this morning, you mean," Jeff said.

Ward said, "Them people were scared out of their minds- all huddled up together over there like we were gonna jump them or something. What was that all about?"

"Notice," Fred said, "the sheriffs came all the way from the Parish- got them out of the Convention Center in a hurry. You know they were not gonna let them white folks stay around us too long. Another thing, we have been in this funky place for days and have not seen a policeman, fire person, or anybody else down here to get us out of here or to help us out. What does that tell you? They don't give a rat's ass about us."

"Look guys," I said, "I have not heard of any plans the government has of getting us out of here. I don't know if they have any plans at all. The way the government and the city have treated us we may as well be on our own."

"Look Mister Smitty," Henry said, "I didn't want to jump into your conversation with those people. They looked scared enough and you looked like you had everything under control. From what we could see you were just letting them vent. Letting them get it all out. We know you were trying to talk to the lady– we picked up on what was going on. We did not want to ruin it for you. But that old man didn't know what the hell he was talking about. First of all here he is coming down here with all that 'colored' shit. Where in the hell he coming from?"

HENRY

Those whites did not give us shit. Look man, I was born in Fazendeville. That place is part of my history.

What the old heads told us was Mr. Jean Pierre Fazende Sr., a free man of color, owned that property. Like in 1856 he gave the property to Jr. Jean Pierre Fazende who began to sell lots to other free people of color, and in 1861 sold lots to ex-slaves. In 1867 these independent property owners formed a Black township. It may well have been the first African American township in Louisiana, if not the south. They had a couple of grocery stores. Our school went to the 9th grade like all the other schools around. We had our church, Battle Ground Baptist Church. I will be the first to admit we had our faults. But there were white towns no better than ours. The big thing was they wanted to take us down.

In 1961 the government and the state wanted to join the Chalmette National Cemetery with the Chalmette Monument. The problem was that Fazendeville cut straight down the middle of the properties. No questioned asked- everybody knew what had to happen if the merger was to be completed. Fazendeville had to go and they knew it.

The Corps of Engineers, the state, St. Bernard, and other interested parties were invited to the closed-door meetings. So many of the meetings were held as far away as Washington, DC. Fazendeville was never invited to any of the meetings. In 1963 the President signed a bill to take the Fazendeville property owners' land. In that action by the president, man, the die was cast for our defeat. They served notice upon us for our immediate removal. In the winter of 1964 Fazendeville was in trouble. All of the houses that were not torn down were bulldozed. We were told the white folks got $20,000 each for their property. Guess what the Blacks got for their property? About $6,000 each. Hey man, that's like a $14,000 rip-off per house and we had something like forty to fifty families who owned properties. Look who got ripped off.

Man, when I heard what that old man said- they paid us too much for our properties- I almost came over there and ruined it for you. I didn't want to mess up what you had going with that lady. Let me tell everybody here and now we have been held hostage ever since they brought us to this country. Understand where I am coming from. They just about took our properties from us! We did not even get half of what the white people got and now the bastards are saying we ripped them off? Our old heads trusted them people too much. You can't give that much power to anybody. That's been our biggest problem all along. But the old people just didn't know. They have been under siege for so long what else could they do? But we younger people, we should have known better. Those white folks have been trying to get us out of the Parish for *a long time and it ain't funny. You can tell that by the way St. Bernard is expanding. Our living history we once had is rapidly dying out. Yet some of our people are trying to keep it alive. Many people found properties in the Lower 9th Ward, some found rentals elsewhere in the city and others just disappeared.*

"Guys I am telling you what I know," Henry finished. "Like so many others, man, I was living that history. Now Fazendeville is gone."

Jeff said, "Let me tell you guys something that been on my mind and on the minds of many other people about how that whole Fazendeville civil rights thing went down."

JEFF

People in the 9th Ward and a few Black people in the Parish told us something had to be done about the way we got ripped off by that forced eviction law the Parish concocted against us. We thought the whole thing had been settled and we had no real nothing to fall back on. We had several meetings at the church and each meeting the church was packed. We wanted to ask the government to investigate the Parish to see if they had violated any of our rights under the new civil rights laws. Reverend Watson, our minister, and leaders as usual agreed to pursue the matter to the end. I know our leaders made some kind of contact with the government, but I don't know the extent of the contact or what kind of reply they got if any.

We were shocked beyond belief when Reverend Watson informed us this white minister and his group from St. Bernard Parish had called for a meeting with our church. Of course we were more than happy to host such a group. We were pleased when the Reverend Bradley, the Parish minister, a couple of lawyer types and some of those good white folks crossed the threshold of our church's door on that very pleasant Wednesday evening. The visitors were greeted in fellowship. The St. Bernard people were amazed by such a large turnout. Our pastor introduced the guests and immediately turned the church over to Reverend Bradley. Minister Bradley gave a short talk in which he asked for forgiveness of any wrongdoing on the part of the people in the Parish. He added that forgiveness must start on both sides if we are to achieve real brotherhood. "As you know we, the Parish people, have always tried to do our best."

All of our members were clapping and agreed with what the minister from the Parish had to say. The lawyer said, "I am here to lay to rest any and all misgivings you good folks might have about the property settlement the Parish made to you people in the acquisition of the Fazendeville property." Some of these comments from the legal man did not go down too well with many of our church people. Several of our church leaders spoke and all of them thanked the white folks for this great and unique meeting. None of them raised any questions on the issues we had the meeting about. Our beloved Pastor Watson spoke briefly. He thanked the visitors for their farsightedness in bringing this wonderful group of people together.

He said this must be a first meeting of its kind anywhere in the community. In this inspirational moment Pastor Watson declared the healing had begun. "This day," he said, "is a milestone in reconciling any lingering differences which may exist, and above all signals a renewed interest in a better race relationship between our two communities." As we all held hands with bowed heads, Reverend Bradley thanked all of us with some parting words and a few hugs as they politely marched their way through the front door.

Several members said, "Whatever this meeting was all about, we felt left out. We didn't know what was going on." A group of us met with the pastor and asked, "What was this meeting really all about?" We told him this goodwill stuff just did not cut it with us. "We wanted to hear from you."

Pastor Watson was quiet for a moment. Then he said, "You members were all at the meeting. You folks saw what went on. This was a good and productive meeting. A first of its kind in the Lower 9- we brought down some old standing barriers and opened the doors of good will. I can tell you most of our members at that meeting will agree to that." As we left the vestry, Pastor Watson looked at each of us and without hesitation said, "I don't know what else to tell you folks. Now excuse me," as he quietly drove away.

Some of our members asked, "How did we make out with the pastor?"

I said, "We got nothing but a lot of sweet talk. It was like case closed."

Melvin said, "Look we told you church people some time ago that the meeting with the white folks was a sham and you little people got shut out of the deal."

We talked with Miss Lucy and she said there was this housekeeper lady who lived back of town near the swamp- she could help clean up this thing. She couldn't be hard to find- not many people live back there.

We found the lady, Miss Bell, who worked for this big army officer in the barracks. She lived on the premises and on her day off she would come to her house on Andry Street. Miss Bell said, "The army people, Minister Bradley, and the big people from St. Bernard used to have dinner at his house several times a month. The talk around the dinner table was the people in Chalmette were frightened of any civil rights action on the part of the Negroes from Fazendeville. One of these people said, 'We don't want the government sneaking around asking these Negroes questions on how much we paid them in the property takeover. We have enough problems already with that damn civil rights situation hanging over our heads. This Fazendeville thing got to be stopped,' he said.

"One of the men said, 'I am sure Pastor Watson will help us out. He worked all those years for us at the slaughterhouse. After all, the pastor looked to us to help him put his church together.'

"Another said, 'Any number of those boys still work for us at the refinery.'

"Minister Bradley said, 'I will call the pastor, set up a good will meeting, and tell him this is the kind of coming together we should have had long ago. Pastor Watson and his people will agree that such a meeting is a good thing

for his people.' The Minister said, 'They all know they owe us a lot.'

Hearing Miss Bell's story, it finally dawned on a few of us what the meeting was all about: shutting down any plans we had about suing the Parish. It didn't have anything to do with this good will shit. It was all about the money. The white folks got what they came for.

Melvin said, "You guys have already figured it out- we, the little people, as usual got nothing."

Jeff continued, "Well guys, I am telling you what I feel and what I know like so many other people- that place was our living history and they took that from us. Fazendeville is gone forever.

Hey everybody, meet Smitty. We met a time or two before the storm and we hooked up a couple days ago. We knew some of the same people back in the day," Jeff said.

"Nice talking to you, but I have to go."

Larry said, "Man, looks like my man Jeff been carrying this pain deep inside for a long time. You got to figure it out. Man this race hurt thing, they whipped on us, we may never shake. You gotta know how to live with this shit or in the long run it will take you down."

Larry said, "Smitty, we know you got to go. Keep it strong and live long." I heard that and moved on.

XVI

SISTER, SISTER

The people in this citadel of opulence to Black achievement looked like victims of a political forced migration with no right of return. A passerby said, "With no help from the government, our city, or anybody else, we are on our own. What can we do? We have nothing. Some people with only the clothes on their backs."

Another said sadly, "Mister, it looks like the tide in our battle for human survival is running against us. What else can we do except hold onto whatever little hope we have left? Mister, we are slaves just looking for a little human dignity in the land of the free."

Some lady in the crowd yelled out, "Mark my words we will never get it."

I looked around at all the sadness, hope bit by bit fading away on the faces of many people. Suddenly a shrill, screaming voice shouted, "Smitty! Smitty! Over here! Is that you?"

"Yes, where are you?"

"Over here, in the corner," she said. After stepping and stumbling over some people I was very much surprised to see, of all people, these two old ladies, Elaine and Estelle, who lived in a big house around the corner from us. Rumor has it that their house was built by their granddaddy and daddy in the late 1890s and early 1900s.

"What in the world are you ladies doing in a place such as this? I thought you told me about a week ago that you were going to a hotel?"

"You know Smitty," Estelle, the older sister, said, "Every time we had to evacuate we checked into the same hotel. We have been doing this for some years and never had a problem. Like everybody else we thought we would be here for a couple of days and go back home. Yet the manager called everyone into the dining room and explained to all of us that the Fire Marshall ordered the entire hotel evacuated and the Marshall wanted everyone out by noon the next day. The manager said the hotel would accommodate everyone that night with no cost to us, but we had to be out by twelve the next day. 'The other hotels in the downtown are being evacuated also. We will provide transportation if you don't have any. We will not take anyone to the Superdome, that's all I'm going to say about that place. We will get you to the Convention Center and if you have transportation we will give you directions. We don't want you to get bogged down on any of these streets.'"

I asked, "Did you all try to get to Houston? I heard that's where people are going."

"Remember," Estelle said, "They told us the sheriff and the police closed all the roads and highways going through Jefferson Parish unless you live there or were with some officers of the law. I wish we could have gotten there from what we have suffered. We drove some people from the hotel over here with us. We could not believe what we saw.

"Some people were running and screaming. They said some people were fighting and one of them pulled a gun. It looked like there were thousands of people. We could not see the fighting and we could not see any weapons. There were so many we figured some violence could break out at anytime. We were in a terrible situation. We walked into this place and it smelled worse than one of those old fashioned outhouses. We all started weeping and crying. We were shedding tears like children. Some people came over, helped us out and calmed us down somewhat. We must properly thank them. They have been kind of keeping an eye on us old ladies. When we get ready to leave here if we ever do we will certainly give them a little something. We may be getting used to the stinkiness of this place," Estelle said.

Elaine said, "Maybe you but not me."

Estelle continued, "Smitty, this place is frightening. We thought our car was parked in a safe place. When we went to check on the car it was a wreck. They had stripped the car down to the bare frame. Everything was gone. They put the car up on tree stumps, took the tires, even the spare. They took the doors, windshields, the engine, and everything they could carry away. When they got through taking everything they set the car on fire. At first I was angry- so very angry. Ever since I saw the car I have lived under total fear. I just can't seem to get away from all the fear. I am not only afraid, but I am scared for every inch of my life and the life of my sister."

"I say to my sister," Estelle continued, "What in God's name is the matter with these Negroes down here? Why are they so bent on destroying themselves and all of us with them? This craziness goes on all day and all night. It never stops. Smitty, I am trying to hold onto what little precious life I have left. I don't want to die in this dirty, filthy, stinky mess of a place. I deserve to die in a better place than this. The Lord knows I have been a long and faithful servant. I have bared my cross without faulting. And in my darkest hours I did my duty without complaint. I have stood the test of time and earned what has been promised to me- my crown. My friend, I want to leave with dignity. I want to die at home."

I really had so little to say, so I said, "If you keep in mind what you have in mind, you, your sister, and your friends will return home with all the grace and honor you have been seeking. Please accept my regards. If all goes well, I will try to get this way tomorrow."

I continued, "How is your brother? I would like to see Darryl one of these days. When we were kids we used to talk a lot about what we were going to do when we grew up. He was such a handsome guy- all the girls liked him a lot. I didn't have a chance with the girls, you know."

Estelle said, "I think about you guys a lot."

ESTELLE

I remember only too well that special morning we were all in church waiting the news. At twelve after 10 AM we were told that God had delivered unto us a boy- Darryl, our brother. For ten Sunday mornings in a row we rang the church bell twelve times to acknowledge the birth of a future minister. We all hoped that our brother would grow up to become a minister like our father and grandfather. Ministering to God's will runs deep in our family. The entire church was joyful of the promise of his youth. He was guided very well towards his future avocation. We spared no effort to take care of our brother as any family would. Darryl married a daughter of the Church, a wonderful young lady, Gloria, from a God-fearing family. Out of that union came two daughters and a fine son.

Greg, our nephew, was raised under the guiding hand of a loving father. My brother and his son walked to church and we rode in the family automobile. All could see the father and son relationship was beaming with happiness. Greg was such a handsome boy- tall and slender with chiseled features. He was the spitting image of his dad, a quiet boy and a good student. He spent a lot of time with books and loved the outdoors. Greg would often visit the bayou, checking plants and life in the swamp. It was not unusual for him and his friends to pick berries at the east end of the swamp.

"The problem," Greg said, "too many people know about the place and it is now always overrun with berry pickers. We found a place close to Arabi' he said, 'just on the other side of the railroad tracks where the picking is great. We go there all the time,' he told us, 'and sometimes I go by myself."

My nephew always got our permission if he was going to the swamp or to pick berries. His dad and granddad were doing some work at the church to get it ready for Sunday morning services. I knew my brother and dad would not be back before dinner. The boy was usually back just before dinner.

For this time of day the humidity was not as high as usual. The sun was down a few degrees and was not that burning hot. It looked like we were in for a very nice evening. The sun was about to meet the horizon, yet my nephew had not returned home. I thought he could have stopped at his friend's house, but normally he would come home and then we would take him over to his friend's house. I said to myself, I bet he's at the church with his dad and granddad. He has got to be there. Where else could he be? But what if he is not there? I went to the sand lot where they played baseball. I didn't want to look too anxious so I took a few seconds to compose myself. A couple of his friends saw me and came over to the car. I asked if they had seen Greg.

One boy said, "I just got here."

"Greg," the other boy said, "was not at the swamp or at the berry patch."

He must be at the church, I thought. Where else could he be? When I got to the church my brother came over. "Hi Sis," he said.

"I came to get your son."

"He is not here. He is probably still at the swamp or on his way home," Darryl said. "Let's go get him and bring him home. That will ease your concerns."

Dad said, "My son and daughter are leaving me without telling me!"

"No!" I said, "We were just going to pick up your grandson and get him home for dinner."

I did not want to tell either of them I was beginning to feel more than a little afraid. I didn't want them saying, "You shower the boy too much." My brother would say, "Let him grow up. He has to become a man in his own right. Now, Sis, you know he has the hands of a man to guide him."

The sun had fallen halfway below the horizon. It was well into the evening when we began driving towards the swamps.

We walked from Caffin between the Florida Canal and the railroad tracks down past Tupelo Canal. We saw nothing. We even went behind Jackson Barracks and looked cautiously a little bit into Arabi. We both knew the boy had better sense than to go into Arabi. We backtracked and covered the Black Horse Ranch from Galvez to Florida and from Tupelo to Dubreuil Streets. We found nothing- not a trace. We did see three children

*playing on the sidewalk. We went over to talk to them.
Before we got close they broke and ran inside.*

*As we approached the house, I saw a lady peeping
from behind the curtains. She saw us, closed the curtain,
turned out the light, and did not answer the door. We
were a little afraid- it was getting dark and a long walk to
the car. The Black Horse Ranch was unsafe in daylight
and was no place to be at night.*

*When we got back, Greg was not home. We went
straight to the fifth precinct police station at St. Claude
and Poland.*

*We were told a missing person report could not be
filled within 72 hours. We told the officer we felt that foul
play was involved here, but we had no proof. Officer
Hartley said, "You have no proof of any kind of foul play.
There is nothing we can do under these circumstances. I
will write this up, leave it for the morning shift and see if
they want to do anything about it. They start work at 7
AM. It is best if you get here just before the shift starts."*

*"We will be here," my brother said. We were there
the next morning when the new shift was checking in.
Darryl talked to the duty officer in charge. My brother
told him his son did not come home last night.*

Captain Hanson said, "I don't have the staff to send out on a case such as this. This is not even a case. My guys are already overloaded. He did not come home last night- is that what you are saying? There might be something to look into. Let's see if I have a guy who could just go out and talk to a few neighbors." He came back and said, "Hold on- I just may have an off-duty officer who may want to go. You will have to wait an hour or so."

The captain made it clear that his officer was there to talk only to a few neighbors and return to the station. So we went back to the house in the Black Horse Ranch. We saw the kids playing. They did not run this time- they got their grandmother. Officer Hyde asked if he could ask her a few questions.

The woman, Mrs. Hall, said, "Officer Hyde, I don't want to get involved in any investigation. It's bad enough living back here. I don't want to be involved in anybody else's problems. I don't want any trouble."

Officer Hyde said, "Miss, I don't want to give you any trouble, just a question please. Did you see anything different back here yesterday that you care to tell us about?"

Before she could answer, the little girl said, "The sheriffs were up there by the railroad."

Mrs. Hall said, "We always hear gunshots up there by the tracks. Lots of young white boys go up there above the tracks to hunt and shoot and whatever behind the pumping stations. I saw three sheriff cars and the coroner's van up there."

Officer Hyde said, "We just may have a jurisdictional problem here. Those gates and all of those things beyond the pumping station may be in the Parish. We better let the captain take a look at this."

When we got back to the station the captain said, "I know the guys over there. Let me make a call and see what is going on over there. From what my officer is telling me this looks out of our hands. But let me check."

I said to my brother, "The captain has been gone a long time. I wonder what is going on. I hope he has not forgotten about us."

Captain Hanson called Officer Hyde into his office and they talked for some time. We were called in. The captain said, "There are several problems. The Parish has the remains of a young Black male. They want to see if you can identify him as your son. The jurisdictional problems can be handled after a positive identification is made. The Parish said they were positive of their jurisdiction in this matter. I told him we were not certain of that until we review the records. The medical examiner's card is at the desk," Captain Hanson said.

As we approached the Parish line I got weaker and weaker. I didn't want to see what I had been thinking. I said to my brother, "That lady whose house we were at yesterday, she has been on my mind all night. She was scared out of her wits and I got the feeling it wasn't because the policeman was with us. I guess there was something else wrong, and being down here in the Parish I would be scared too.'

"She does not live in the Parish. That house is in the Black Horse Ranch. That's New Orleans," Darryl said. "Well, we are here. Let's go in." We were introduced to Dr. La Beau, the medical examiner. Sadly, we met all the conditions necessary to make a positive identification that the body was that of my nephew. My brother asked Dr. La Beau, "How soon can we get my son's body?"

The examiner hesitated. "We will call you tomorrow morning and you can probably remove the body in the evening, or at the latest, early the next morning. The sheriff investigation will be completed before the end of the week. You will be invited to this informal inquiry. Let me assure you folks, all of the facts will be on the table for your examination at that time. Since the investigation is ongoing we are unable to give any details. We will call your family tomorrow," La Beau said.

I said to my brother, "If that home is in New Orleans, why is Mrs. Hall so afraid?"

Darryl said, "Let's go and find out."

When we got there she let us in without any hesitation. My brother said, "The sheriff found the body of my son over there. My sister would like to ask you for some details if you are willing."

"Look Mister," Mrs. Hall said, "We live way back here in the Black Horse Ranch. The NOPD never comes back here unless we call them. They take their own good time to get to us. You would think the way the sheriffs act that we are in the Parish. They come back here, pick up these young Black boys all the time, and charge them with whatever they want to. They keep them in jail until they decide to let them out. The New Orleans Police don't say anything other than, "We will look into the matter." That is all you will ever hear about that. The sheriffs and the other white folks go back there to shoot target practice all the time. They don't go back there to hunt. They go back there to shoot. These young white boys are there almost every evening shooting up the place."

Mrs. Hall continued, "You don't want to be back here when they have one of those drinking parties on the weekends. We can't sit on our own front porch. Those bullets are flying all over the place. Mister, I understand your hurt about the death of your son, and no doubt you want to see justice done for your son. But you must understand, I am a grandmother, as you can see, with three grandchildren - two boys and a girl - and no man in the house. I am struggling hard enough. Now what do you think will happen to my grandchildren if something happens to me? Those white folks in the Parish will think nothing about destroying what little family we have left. I have seen it done back here before. Mister, I will tell you everything I saw and I will not lie to you. But I will not testify on your behalf against any of those young white boys in St. Bernard Parish. It is out of the question. Miss, if you or your brother is thinking about my testifying we can stop this right now."

Darryl said, "All we want is to hear what you have to say."

"I did not see your son go up to the tracks or around the building. Three young white boys came with guns and six packs. They did some drinking and shooting as usual. Your son came from around the building with his back to them and he was headed like he was going into the berry *patch. One boy raised his gun and shot the boy in the back. The other two shot your son also. The boys jumped in their car and sped away. A very short time later the sheriff came with the boys, the coroner, and an older man, who came in a separate car. They did not waste any time taking the boy's body away. Later that evening you and your brother came. The body had already been taken away. Someday, I may have to answer in judgment for not testifying for you. Why did I have to witness such a tragic event? Only the Lord knows."*

Darryl said, "There may be some help for us at the NOPD. They probably would want to look at their final report."

Mrs. Hall looked at us with a frown of disgust on her face. She said, "Mister, I don't trust these people in St. Bernard, and you better not trust those in New Orleans. Mister, don't you know all these white people sip soup out of the same cup?"

As we drove home we did not know what to make of the warning she just gave us. Greg's body had been released to our family and the time for the inquiry had been set. At the inquiry Dr. La Beau stated that, "This is not a formal inquest and the rules thereof do not apply. Our only purpose is to announce the findings of the investigation. I will read these conclusions from this combined report."

Darryl stood up and said, "You mean my son was killed and I can't even ask who killed my son and how many took part in his killing?"

Dr. La Beau said, "Sit down and be quiet. You can't ask any questions before or after I finish reading the report."

Darryl said, "Mister, you told us all the facts would be on the table for our examination. Now you are telling us we can't get the facts and we can't ask any questions?"

"You got that right, boy. I am not going to tell you again to sit down and shut up."

That was too much for my brother. Darryl said, "I came down here to get some answers and some answers I want to get."

Dr. La Beau said, "You will get what I will give you. I am telling you for the last time, sit down and shut up. You don't know whom you are talking to."

Darryl said, "Yes, I know whom I am talking to!"

Dr. La Beau blew up, saying, "But you damn sure don't know where you are!"

Darryl shouted back, "Yes, I know who you are and what you are and I know where I am!"

Mr. La Beau said, "Boy, you are just another one of them low down troublemakers. We got your kind down here in the Parish. You people are the cause of all of our problems. You can bet your life, and I said bet your life, we are going to take care of them and we are going to take care of you before I am through. You hear me boy? You mean you came down here and disrespected me and expect to walk away from here? Not on your life. You really don't know where the hell you are. I will keep your Black ass in jail until hell freezes over. You can count on that!"

Before I knew it, my brother was handcuffed with his hand behind his back, standing between two sheriffs and a sheriff standing behind the examiner's desk. The older white man who was there with a young teenage boy went over to the examiner and whispered something to him. They went into the outer office. When they came back the examiner said, "Take the cuffs off and we will take a twenty minute recess." The older man said the coffee bar was down the hall, "Just make sure to be back in twenty minutes."

As we walked to the coffee bar I said, "It will not do you or the family any good if you go to jail. We will not get justice down here so we will listen to what he has to say and take it to the next level. Some justice might be found in New Orleans. We will go to the police department and the DA's office and see if there is anything they can do."

Dr. La Beau read the entire report, and what he said in essence was that my nephew died in an accidental death of bullet wounds to the upper torso by a single party or parties unknown. That was the official conclusion- case closed.

We only invited the immediate family members to the burial. It was at the gravesite where my brother stated that he would remain at the site to be with his son for just a few moments longer. Elaine and I were the last ones to leave. As our brother prayed the only words we could clearly hear were, "My son... My son... Great God almighty you have taken my only son."

We met with the New Orleans authorities that had talked with the Parish. The Parish insisted they had jurisdiction in the matter. The case was closed. As we walked south away from the building, my brother looked at me and said, "The old lady, Mrs. Hall, who lives down in the Black Horse Ranch said," as he looked back at the building, "they all sip soup out of the same cup. Don't they?"

I looked at Estelle. "The first time I saw you and your sister since I got back was just before the storm. I did not see your brother. I wanted to ask you about him and his family. I left at such an early age I lost track of so many of them. I don't know just where to start looking for them. But there are just three or four of the old friends I would really like to see. Your brother is one of them. So how are things going with him?"

Estelle said, "Smitty, as you may have been told, me and my sister have never married. We spent most of our lives looking out for and taking care of our brother. When Darryl's only son met with that so-called accidental death, (they murdered Greg, you know), our family became closer to his wife and children. If his family needed our help we were there for them. We wanted him to know as his older sisters we would be there for him. Whom else could he turn to?

"Gloria, his wife, told us in a strong, firm voice, 'Your brother is not acting like a man with a family.' We told her if she needed any assistance we would be here for her. Gloria said, 'We should not have to come to you or your sister to do what my husband should be doing. Taking care of his family is his responsibility. It is not about you giving us money. In case you don't know it, it's all about having a man in the house taking care of his family duties. I can't do it on my salary alone. We have two girls to raise. I need a man in the house.'

"We saw his wife become distant. She finally moved to DC and took the girls with her. Let me tell you, his wife gave him little support while he was going through the agony of his son's death. He did his best to be a good father and would have been a good husband if she had only worked with him. From what we saw day to day, he was handling his problems as all God fearing people would. But from time to time I felt a slippage in the righteousness of his behavior," Estelle said.

I said to her, "I really don't know Darryl's wife or his children. I would like to meet them someday if we ever get out of this mess we are in here. But I just want Darryl's telephone number or something. I would like to call him and just talk a little bit. Maybe our meeting can wait."

Estelle paused somewhat, speechless, and in a deep breath she said, "Smitty, dear Smitty, I can't forget that knock- that dreaded knock upon the door. It was a cold, bleak, rainy night. 'You better come,' his buddies warned. 'He has overdosed on that crack or smack.' I don't remember which. When we got there my loving brother lay facedown in a gutter, half filled with muddy water. I held his hand as he was gasping for breath. It was like he just refused to die in a gutter of muddy water.

"We cleaned him, put him in his bed which we kept since he was a boy. It was at the gravesite, I witnessed mother earth embracing my brother as she wrapped her arms around him and gently brought him into her bosom. I was overwhelmed with joy. I began to scream and shout, 'My brother, my brother, my father's only son is on his way to join you.' My suffering was over.

"Smitty, I am glad we spotted you. I know you want to go. But let me say this- at that informal inquest, if you can say that's what it was, the medical examiner said some things that disturbed me until this day. When he said, 'You people are the cause of all our problems,' did he really mean all the problems in the Parish are caused by Black people?"

"I don't know. I was not there to hear what he had to say. But it sounds to me like he was making some pretty broad condemnations. It is as if he was not only putting Black people in St. Bernard at risk but all of us everywhere."

She said, "Some Blacks who live down there say the jail is filled with Black people. Some church members say they only send Black prisoners to the New Orleans Parish jail where their families can't find them. We have a very small number of Black people who live in St. Bernard, yet the jail in the Parish is full of young Black males. I finally figured it out. These people are in control of everything. How are we ever going to get a fair hearing from any of them? I don't see how in the name of the Almighty these white people can misuse us for so long and continue to do so. We are all supposed to be children of the same God. They know all of us bear witness to the same faith, but more times than not they treat us as inhumans with no faith and no God at all. Our faith, as the Almighty knows, is solid as the rock and our belief runs deeper than the deepest sea. We can't let them lay all the guilt at our feet, as they have always done, for the destruction of the Black community. I know we have to take our share of the blame. We got to do a better job if we want our young boys to grow up and function as Black men should," Estelle said.

Elaine said, "We know you don't like to hug but we have known you long enough. We are going to take a hug each!" We hugged and I moved on.

XVII

The Army Runs out of Food

There was so much movement in the Center about twenty-five of us were able to find space in a good spot up against the wall right next to the stairway. In case of a problem we could always take the stairs and go through the dining area or the kitchen and exit onto the opposite street. This was a good way out just in case we could not get out the front doors. We secured the area and assigned volunteers to take turns keeping their eyes on all our properties. We all agreed.

Suddenly, we heard a bunch of noise. James came up and said, "The army came in and set up a food distribution center near the end of this very narrow street. How come the army set up the food give-away on this narrow-ass street?"

Harry said, "Man, we gotta have at least 10,000 people down here. They will never feed all of us and have this thing done by nighttime. Look there is something else going on with these people. Let's see how this thing plays out. You know if some bad shit happens lots of people gonna be trapped down here."

"Yep, you are right," James said. "It's hard to estimate but it looks like about less than 1,000 people have plates in their hands. It is really hard to know."

The army announced, "We have run out of food. We will not be back."

James said, "Bam. Closed up shop in record time and on their way."

I felt that with such quick action and so many angry, hungry people some kind of holy hell would be coming down. As soon as the shut-down came, people started throwing rocks, bricks, and whatever they could find. They had no real target in mind. It helped that so few things could be found to be used as weapons. So many of us bystanders began to find safe shelter as best we could. In spite of the shouting and screaming and the punches thrown, the people on the whole seemed somewhat calm in keeping this thing from getting out of control. In fact, another thing that helped was that Ben and Billy and some people went directly into the center of this action and they were screaming with hands in the air, "Cool it man, cool it," and they were saying that, "All these people want us to do is fight amongst ourselves, man."

Several other people were shouting, "Listen up people, listen up everybody." So many around us began to listen up. Ben said, "You mean to tell us they didn't know how many of us we have back here? They knew up front that little bit of shit ass food wasn't gonna feed all of us. You mean the army didn't know that and they closed it down? 'Screw you,' the army man said, and, 'We are out of here!' Man, these people will do anything to get us to destroy ourselves. They will be ever grateful if we would just do the job for them. Keep in mind all the fighting among ourselves is the first down payment of the Man taking this city back. It looks like to me from what little news and stuff coming our way they are forcing us out of here and sending us everywhere we don't want to go."

Eddy said, "In this place right here they got us on lockdown. They are gonna ship so many of us out of this city when you look down upon it, it will look like our city is covered with one, long, big white sheet. Without a doubt there will be Black in the mix, but they won't be like us. They will be lean, clean and green."

On leaving that part of the Center, we connected with a few people we had met at one of the other stops. We talked a little bit. We all seemed to be of the opinion that with so many angry, hungry people it was remarkable that some greater disturbance did not occur. These people did act pretty good.

XVIII

KIDS & SEGREGATION

Most people in the group came back looking for a good spot to settle in for the evening. I picked a place against the wall directly in front of the stairs. It had a good vantage point with a clear view of the front doors and an easy exit up the stairs just in case. Some people checked out the toilet paper and we had plenty. All kinds of food were being exchanged and we, too, shared food and supplies with a few people who got shut out from the food distribution. By this time we must have had about twenty-five or so people in the group. After the usual loud and somewhat preachy conversation, we saw this lady looking around and moving in all directions as if she was looking for someone or something. We didn't know what was going on. She approached us and asked, "Could we join your group?"

Billy said, "What we? Where is this we?"

She said, "I will go get them. They are over there." When she came back she said, "These are my three children, all boys. Brad is thirteen, the oldest, he loves sports as do all boys his age. Sean is eleven, the in-between one, mom's straight A student, wants to be a lawyer when he grows up. He loves to read and asks a lot of questions.

Most of them I can't answer. Ray, my baby, will be ten on October 20th. He likes to work in gardens and grow things. I hope that will lead to something good. Well, as long as he is happy. I am Lakendra, their mother, as most of you already know."

Everyone said, "Bring them on in." The lady said that she was a cousin to the cousin-in-law of that person over there. They both agreed. She went on to say her group had split up. Some were going to the parking lot at the Dome and others wanted to get to the Airline Highway where they would be picked up and taken to the airport.

She said, "With three children I didn't want to take that kind of a chance, so I stayed in the Center and here I am. We don't have any food. My children have not eaten for a while. They are real hungry by now. We had a little food late last night and a couple cookies this morning."

Daniel said, "Lady, we have all the goodies you and the boys can eat. Brought from that damn give-away. Lady we have whatever you need tucked away in our coolers." A couple ladies went over to help them with the food.

Bart said, "What are we gonna do with all of the good stuff when they come to take us away, man?" with a slight laugh.

Daniel's voice was heard saying, "I don't know and I don't give a rat ass. Let's break bread with the hungry."

After they ate, these kids added a renewed energy to the group. In the group there were several of the usual conversations going on at the same time as the kids looked and listened intently. The kids seemed amazed at what was going on and were enjoying themselves being with adults. As the conversation became somewhat relaxed, Sean, one of the kids, looked at me and said, "Mister can I ask you a question?"

"Sure you can."

He said, "Mister, what was segregation like down here when you were a kid?" This was the kind of shock I was not ready to handle. The question coming from such a young boy silenced the noise of the group. I became a bit unsettled. I don't ever remember talking to a kid about segregation. I didn't know what to say, but I wanted to say something. After a few brief moments I said to myself, *whatever you want to say, take your time and frame the conversation with the words an eleven-year-old can understand.*

"Let me give you a brief summary without going into real details in answering your question. Perhaps we can have a deeper conversation into this matter once we have this evacuation thing settled. It is common knowledge that if we want to get any understanding of segregation we must examine the institution of slavery. You will stay on track in your understanding as long as you keep in mind that slavery was a criminal and immoral enterprise. The institution of slavery was legalized by the state, the government, and above all sanctioned by the Church. Slaves were forbidden to practice their own African religions. In order to completely make the slave into a non-person, the master had to destroy all traits of everything culturally good about Africa. In so many cases he did. The irony was the only religion the slave could practice openly was Christianity. The slave master exploited our bondage to its ultimate place- that an animal could not in its own right be free. Slavery was therefore forever, without the right of freedom or the possibility of redemption.

"By all human accounts we are human beings, yet the white slave master completely destroyed our families. It was a common business practice for him to sell the children. The boys were sold to the highest bidder. The father or mother was most likely sold separately. The slave girls were kept by the slave master for breeding purposes to replace the slaves sold or for his personal pleasure. The white master said there was nothing personal in what he did. It was all business. Business is the American Way.

"The Church declared Blacks from Sub-Saharan Africa to be heathens and the slave master took that to mean that those slaves were stock and trade. Only Black people could be put into slavery. In carrying out the idea of producing a non-person he gave us new names and identities that were of his own creation. In other words, we were made over into what he called 'the new Negro.' Our African cultures, our mores, and the greatness that was once ours, may well have been destroyed forever. Louisiana, with other southern states, rebelled to maintain and expand their slave-holding society. The South lost the war of rebellion. Back in 1865 it looked like we were on the doorstep of small bit of freedom. But that small bit of freedom was not to be ours for very long. Louisiana and the Confederate states never intended for us to be a free people. Their aim was to put us back into slavery, but they couldn't so they created segregation, the next best thing to slavery, which put us in bondage for the rest of our days. The segregationists said, 'Segregation is forever.'

"You must understand that slavery, and its child in crime, were two of the most heinous crimes in all of humankind. There has been no greater crime. After the rebellion was put down, New Orleans, like Louisiana, was under the total control of white people. The segregation laws were made by white men for the protection of white people against Black people. They enforced these laws in the courts and in everyday life in the most brutal and degrading ways imaginable against Black people. Blacks had to accept the status of being a second-class citizen from birth to the day they died. Blacks were trained to put the white man first in everything they did.

"Maybe a few simple examples will suffice. If you were at a bus stop with whites and Blacks, the whites always boarded the bus first. You would never try to get on the bus ahead of the white people. When it was time to get off the bus, white people got off from the front door of the bus and Black people always got off from the back door of the bus.

"Here are a few more examples which you may want to look at. If a white man with or without his family was walking towards you, with or without your family, your family had to step aside and let them pass. The white man always had the right of way in all cases. When a white girl reached a certain age her mother or father would always tell you, 'From now on you address our daughter as *Miss*. You will say *yes Ma'am* or *no Ma'am* as the case may be.' He would say, 'These are the rules and you have to follow them.' Most Black people knew that and followed the rules. When it came to the white boy, the right of passage was involved in the 'Mister' thing- manhood. The father normally left it up to the son when to assert the right of passage. The son would say to you, 'Boy, regardless of your age, from now on you will address me as Mister so and so.' You would say, 'Yes Sir, Mister so and so, I understand.' Once he made that decision he had passed from a boy into manhood.

"Notice one thing. He called that Black man a boy. Remember in the white man's mind that so-called Black boy, however old, would never attain the right of passage into manhood. Some white people have always said the Blacks in New Orleans were a little different and a little bit better off under segregation than most Blacks in the state."

Ben said, "White folks are always telling us how better off *we* are when *they* get everything. Hey man, let me tell you something. A little bit better off is like not being better off at all."

Sean said, "Mr. Smitty, do you think racism will ever end in this country?"

"I will not attempt to answer that question at this time. It's getting late. But what do you think?"

XIX

FALSE ALARM

Things were picking up outside from what we could see. It looked like a busy night was underway. The people were moving around, rather erratically. On the inside the movement was easing for the most part- a sleepy silence had begun to settle in on another dark night. I used my bag as usual for a pillow and put my backpack between my legs for safety and pulled the blanket over me to ward off any coolness of the early morning breeze.

We were awakened about 2:30 AM by the rumbling and tumbling of a noisy fight outside. No one in our group, like others, could sleep through all this commotion. The children slept through it without making a move. About 3:00 AM I was back under my blanket.

Sometime before daybreak we heard these loud, painful, excruciating screams. People were running and shouting- those hollowing screams were coming from everywhere inside and outside the center. They were saying, "The river has broken," and repeating the same thing over and over- "The river has broken! The river has broken! The river has overflowed," they said. "We all gonna drown." This great wave of people was off running in our direction. You could not see beyond them. You could only hear the screaming and that deep, gushing, destructive noise beyond the people. That aggravating sound was becoming all consuming as it got closer and closer to us. People jumped up in fright and ran in all directions.

I had a way out. I quickly ran for the stairs. I made my way to the top of the stairs when I hit an invisible wall. I was trapped. In a brief moment of escape I turned, looked down the stairs, and gazed at the three boys asleep on the floor. I could not imagine their fate as the disaster was approaching. I tried to take a step down the stairs toward the boys but before I could complete the step several shouting voices said, "They are helicopters! They are helicopters! The river is not broken. Everything is ok," they said.

It all happened so fast and so quickly I did not know what to think. I was not feeling ok. I began to worry how I could have run off and have left those three children to die. That was not me, and I am convinced of that. I have always wanted to be too deeply involved in humankind to let anything like that happen.

I said to Doris, the lady standing on the steps next to me, "If I am what I just did, there is something wrong deep inside me. I have to find out what went wrong in me."

Doris said, "Did you take anything with you when you ran for the stairs?"

"Yes. I grabbed my backpack and ran up the stairs."

She said, "Mister, you grabbed your backpack and ran up the stairs, but you didn't grab the children, right? You just left the children there to die. Now you want us to tell you what kind of person you are? Yes, we know the kind of brother you are," Doris said. "If you would just let the things inside of you seep to the surface, you too will know the kind of person you are." She descended the stairs without looking back.

XX

THE WATCHFUL EYE

I couldn't stop thinking about how I had betrayed the three little boys on the Convention Center floor. But I was about to find out about my own betrayal.

"Hello Mister you still here?" Miss Agness asked.

"Yes ma'am I'm still here."

"You ain't no genius son, and you ain't got no eyes in the back of your head." She continued, "I told you to keep your eyes open and your ears to the ground and you will learn a lot. I heard your cousin making plans last night. You were counted out before they talked with you. Pam said she did not want to abandon you, she wanted to give you a chance to back out on your own. She said you seem to always have some kind of back up plan. Nevertheless she did not want anything to get back to the family that your word was not considered. That would not have set well with the family- she made that very clear. What you have to understand Mister is they never made any plans of going to Houston or any place like that. She told them last night she could take three months off before she had to go back to the office. After all, she said, she has been in the government for nearly twenty-five years. She is about right on that. I have known Pam for some time. They all were gonna show up across that river in Algiers so they can get involved in their rituals. In all that stuff they are doing they are bowing down to the wrong God.

"Listen Mister, aside from all of that, didn't you see how close that Merelyn from down the hall and your cousin were couched together? Your dear cousin and that sister been hooked up together for a long, long time. Let me tell you what I know and God loves the truth. It used to be back at the old apartment before that lady got herself a boyfriend, and I know that boyfriend stuff weren't gonna last too long. After everyone had gone to bed I used to peep on your cousin tiptoeing down the hall with a light tap on the door like she was going in some speakeasy. And she didn't leave until the early hour of the morning sometimes. Daybreak caught her coming out the door. They didn't know anybody was watching but I kept a close eye on things.

"Your cousin would often say to me they practice what they call 'Nonsectarian Dualism.' She said there are two sides of everything and everything has two, if you know what I mean. I don't know what you call all those shenanigans they are doing but in the eyes of the Almighty I know it is downright evil. They are gonna have to answer for all their misdeeds. You can mark my word on that.

"Mister I am talking to you as if you are my only son but the Master did not see fit to bless me with a son. He did give me three wonderful daughters and not one of them ever went astray."

I responded, "You know Miss Lady, my cousin's deeds are my cousin's deeds and no one else's. If she can find just a few good people and just a few good vibes along the way, she will have had a wonderful life. Because she is what she is and she ain't what she can't be. Good morning, dear lady."

"Good morning," she said as we both moved on.

We proclaim our righteousness to the highest.

Our brothers and sisters are stopped at the gates of Eternity. "Dead slaves enter through the back gates of Eternity," said the High Gate Keeper. "Eternity is only open to the precious few of the other kind, seldom for any of your kind," remarked the Keeper.

As the dead slaves struggled to enter the Promised Land, we danced and pranced back and forth up on the graves of our dead slaves.

-Uncle Billy talking to his group under the Tree of Knowledge; 1935

Day 6: Friday, September 2, 2005

XXI

THE MAD SUPERDOME

Later on that morning, a few of us walked across the street and Walt said, "What was that helicopter scare all about this morning? It took me by surprise."

Billy said, "It just goes to show you the conditions we are all in. Any little nothing can set the whole place off."

Ben said, "Well, look up the street. What the heck is all that headed our way? Where are all these damn people coming from? It is where they are gonna wind up at that worries me. Folks, looks like we got more company coming to the Center. The more people, the more problems, big time. They don't look too friendly, I can tell you that."

Alice said, "Let's talk to them and feel them out."

We said hi and they said hi and the conversation started. "Where are you people from?" we asked.

Doug, the group leader, said, "That's a long story."

DOUG

Some of us have been down at the Superdome since Saturday. That's when the mayor said it was alright to go down there. When we got there the damn place was closed. More and more people were showing up. They had so many people outside on Saturday they had to let us in. Late Saturday it was like an explosion of people. We knew there was trouble on the way. Some of the people here with us today were there on Saturday- they can tell you themselves. What we did was kind of put ourselves together for our own safety. We held on the best we could. Sunday the shit hit the fan. People were everywhere. The Dome was overrun- no place to go- not a place to hide from the crazies inside and the mob outside. Man, we were trapped. But the real problem was there was not a policeman or fire department, no kind of health services at all. Man, the people downtown knew with all these people violence had to break out.

The violence did not wait until Sunday- it started early Saturday night. You could see these people had guns, knives, and one of these crazies was strutting around the damn place with a machete in clear view of everybody. You know on Sunday, Mister Mayor called for a mandatory evacuation of the entire city. For people coming to the Superdome that order came too late. The Dome had already filled to the brim. When the people showed up in mass and violently pushed their way into the Dome, others had to settle for the parking lots or the streets. Late Sunday night and early Monday morning as the hurricane made landfall the winds picked up and blew two holes in the roof of the place. The government, the state, and the city authorities could not be found. Panic broke out inside and outside.

Some of these people were running around the place shouting and screaming, stealing and shooting guns inside the place until late in the day when the storm was over. All of the toilets were broken and flowing into the place. The stench and sight of the waste were unbelievable. There was no help in sight.

Man, let me tell you all something. From what we were told you people had it pretty good over here at the Center. The whole city knew about the Dome and everybody came. They brought too many problems with them. While the storm was doing its thing, two guys got into it and some other guys joined in and when it was all over one brother lay dead right before our eyes. People were walking around it, or stepping over the body until two old ladies came with a blanket and covered the body. The people who came in on Sunday told us the Lower 9th Ward was hard hit and looks like the whole place is under water. People on rooftops, small homemade rafters, and anything they could hold on to that would float. One guy was even in a tree. That was funny, but it was sad. The *people of the Lower 9 can't hold on much longer. They are desperately in need of help. There were a few boats down there picking up people but there were too many people stranded and not nearly enough boats and rescue people.*

Kevin, another person in their group, said, "People were looting and stealing and all that kind of stuff. Look we were out of food and water. We had to get something to eat. Nobody brought us anything, not one drop of water, not one piece of bread. It looks like they are trying to starve us out. What did they expect us to do? Just lay down and die?"

Eddy from their group said, "That's the plan for us. Just lay down and die."

EDDY

What we were doing, they called it "looting." We called it "marching" to get some food and water for our women and children. Man they want us out of here in the worst kind of way.

Here was the big kisser. The Red Cross wanted to give us some help. You know, food and water and shit. The big bosses told them, "Don't even think about going down to the Dome." This is what we heard late Thursday evening. That was just yesterday. Go tell them don't give us that shit about looting and stealing. Our fricking mayor stopped the police from rescuing the people and turned them on the people! Man, pick up on this- the police was stopping people in the streets and they told us we had to give up our protection if we wanted to go to Houston. When we got to the Dome things were out of order. The whole place was a mess. It was unbelievable and nobody going no place. Even though the police was trying to slick us out of our protections, some of us did not go for the con game they were trying to pull on us. We saw the trick up front- take the weapons and you got the people. We went around telling people not to give up their protection. We don't know where they plan to take us or what they have in store for us.

Folks, we may never get to Houston. We did not know what the government had in store for us, when one of the big muckety mucks dressed in plain clothes said to everyone, "We need you to give up your guns. We want you to turn over all of your guns to the police department. We are doing this for your protection and the safety of New Orleans." Nobody gave up the weapons. The government man said in a more commanding voice, "Under the law of search and seizure we will have the

military and the police confiscate any and all contraband."
He said, "No one will be allowed to board the buses
without first being searched. No one male or female."

From what we could tell he forced several thousand
to yield to his demands. Unless they bring in more trucks
it gonna take a long time to move all those people out of
the Dome.

Gerald, one of the leaders from the Dome, said, "Here is the word in the streets. Last night the government didn't even know there were people at the Convention Center. The street said when the government people found out that you folks had been over here for almost a week with little food and water and no medical care, they went ballistic. Man, the army people and the government man were shouting and cursing all over the place and at each other. The Big Chief told everyone, 'If anything is wrong over there heads are going to roll, and I don't mean maybe.' The army man said, 'Get some food and supplies over there, now that's an order,' he said."

Gerald said, "Some people from the Center came over to the Dome late last night and told us the army had run out of food and they did not know why. We saw a few army trucks with a few soldiers trickling in Thursday late afternoon. They must have been the unit coming to feed you guys."

Doug said, "Look, they are telling us we are going to Houston, but when the truth came down they are sending us all over the country. Nobody is saying anything about how we are gonna get back to New Orleans."

Irvin said, "I ain't leaving New Orleans. This is my home. This is home to all of us. Getting us out of here is the best way of keeping us out of here and our properties are theirs for the picking. To me, they want all of our property. Once we are gone, we ain't coming home. You people who are thinking about going to Houston or any other place, before you get on those buses take a long hard look at the city. It may be the last time you see New Orleans."

Genna said, "What I want to know, early this morning before we got started for the Convention Center, there was a huge explosion."

GENNA

The blast was so big it shook all the way to the Dome. We were out in the lots- we saw the blaze and the sky lit up like a Christmas tree. Then came three other smaller explosions. They were not as big as the first one. They scared the living hell out of us. Later on several of our groups went over and talked to the authorities. They said they would be out shortly to give everybody whatever information they could on the matter. We explained to them people outside as well as in the Dome wanted to know what was going on. The army man said, "We are gathering information," and that he would have a spokesperson out to brief us.

The army spokesperson said all of the explosions were in Chalmette down in St. Bernard Parish and he said that in the information they received no one was seriously injured. He said, "Aside from that, here is the information we have on the evacuation process. The Astrodome and the other centers are running over with people. They cannot take any more evacuees." He also said, "The state will not lend us any of their buses, even after the governor told us we could use them. What we do know," the army man said, "starting tonight and tomorrow morning we will have enough army vehicles here to swing the evacuation into high gear. The people at the Dome will be the first to be evacuated," he said. "We are informing the Center people if they get to the Dome tonight or first thing tomorrow morning we will evacuate them with the people at the Dome. Those of you who are staying in New

Orleans, you will have to find shelter elsewhere in the city. The mayor's orders are to close the Dome within the next week or so."

"Where are all you people gonna go?" Ben from our group asked.

"We ain't gonna go no place," Doug answered. "We are already where we want to be. Home, man. New Orleans."

XXII

PREACHER MAN

While some people were spreading the news about the evacuation plans at the Dome, we noticed three men driving up in a pearly white Cadillac a few car lengths behind the crowd. When he stepped out of the back seat, everyone knew he was not a politician. He must be, we all thought, a licensed preacher. He wore alligator shoes with white linen trousers and a light pale blue silk shirt. And his head was covered with a seldom seen panama hat. In his right hand was a copy of the Word. As he approached the people he opened the book, flipped a few pages, and waved to the crowd with a big "God bless you."

He said in a strong but pleasant voice, "I am guided by the light to help relieve your pain. You have been carrying this burden far too long. I am the Reverend Eugene Leonard Norton, pastor of the Way of the Cross Baptist Church. Those who are familiar with my work call me the Reverend Leonard. We all know the Astrodome is not taking any more evacuees and the Center in Houston is just about out of room. Looking at that grim situation, our church contacted our member church in Houston to join us in this effort to house some of you good people in our centers. Let me make this clear. At the centers there will be no charge no matter how long you good people stay there. Our centers are extensions of God's house. There can be no charge. Look, there is no charge from here to the boat, and in Houston to our centers. No charge. The Church has five buses and they can only hold sixty people each. The only charge is for the boat ride from New Orleans to Houston. Here is the way this thing is going to work. You sign up now, then when you are ready to board the buses you pay our church $40 per person. The church wants to tell you your children ride for free. We are going to leave the young Pastor Brown here to get the list signed and get things organized. We will be back in about an hour at the most. Please be packed and ready to go."

I was watching this with two older ladies, Helen and Joyce. Helen said to me, "This is church works at its best. What do you make of all this?"

I said, "It all looks good to me. If he can get these people to high grounds and a roof over their heads, $40 seems cheap enough. Look at all those people signing up. There must be several hundred of them. They really want to get out of here and I can't blame them."

Helen looked at Joyce and said, "I wonder if that young preacher is any kin to the famed Reverend Leonard. He sure sounds like it."

Joyce said, "I was watching his body language. He set a good mood for these people. This preacher knew what he was doing and he did it well. If you ask me. Just look at the people lined up to go. You can tell he is a man of God. Right now I am not saying much more since I gotta go to the powder room."

"Me too," Helen said. "Mister Smitty, let's see what good news he brings us when our Cadillac man returns. You will be around later, won't you Mr. Smitty?"

"Yeah."

While the preacher was doing his thing, it seemed I was getting an attitude from the ladies as if I did not quite trust the preacher. They may have been right. I just couldn't tell. I really didn't know how this thing was gonna go down. What I did know there could be a lot of money changing hands and if it did not go down right so many poor people would be hurt.

XXIII

PEOPLE OF THE DOME

It was too early to be scorched on this burning, windless Friday morning. Our group wanted to check the action up the street to see if any new word had come down from the Dome about the evacuation plan. We met several groups who had spent the night and most of the morning gathering information in and around the Dome about the evacuation. They were very angry when we spoke to them about the way the government was treating them at the Dome.

They seemed willing to express their anger in the most violent ways. Leon, from the Dome, said, "We have run out of patience with talking. We are out of patience with listening to the Man and all of this BS. We want to get something done, man."

Ralph, a group leader, said, "When you see children who have not eaten for days and older people crying without medicine, food, or help from the government, man, time is up."

Leon and his group were from the East. Leon said, "Our group was back there in the East where the Chef meets 10 freeway. The high water forced us out of there.

We hit the road on Tuesday and we didn't get to the Dome until late Thursday. With all of the army trucks coming and going and the helicopters overhead you would think somebody would have picked us up. But they kept rolling straight on by like we didn't exist."

"You didn't exist to them people," a loud voice shouted. "That's the point you missed."

Ralph said, "We came back over here to tell you what is going down at the Dome. Now here's what the Big Man told everybody: the army convoy will probably not get to New Orleans until late Saturday or early Sunday. The man also said, the Astrodome and all the other centers in South Texas are also closed to new evacuees. Mr. Army Man said they are shipping people out of Houston but he had no information where they were being shipped to. 'But we know that people at the Superdome,' he said, 'will more than likely be shipped to other states around the country. But there is no plan as far as I know to ship you people from the Superdome out of the U.S.'"

Larry said, "This is the kind of shit that got everybody P.O.'d over at the Dome." As the crowd grew more vocal he continued.

These people are shipping us all over the country. Don't be surprised if some of us don't wind up in some foreign country. We all know what our so-called government did to us and to the Indians. They rounded them all up and made them walk three thousand miles, never to return, just like they picked us up and brought us here. And they told all of us, "Forget about any kind of Right of Return." That is what is called the get-even plan. Get them out and never get them back. Katrina was made for these people. It served us up on a gold platter for them.

Mister, we want you and the government to know the people in our group ain't leaving. New Orleans is our home and we have every right to be here. We told them there are thousands of people stranded at the Convention Center. We said, "What are you all gonna do about those people?"

The new spokesperson for the army said, "What people?" He said strongly, "We have no knowledge of any people at the Center." They said, "Our primary concern is the evacuation of the Superdome. The National Guard may have an interest in the people at the Center but we have no knowledge to that extent."

I said to the government man, "We heard all last night the mayor floating the idea that since the Astrodome and the other places in Houston are filled to the limits, the mandatory evacuations could be lifted for the time being. He said the people could go or stay if they wanted to." The government man said he heard something along those lines but nothing official.

Helen and Joyce were back and had brought some other people with them. We all greeted each other and they joined the group. Our group had now expanded to about fifty strong.

Jack from the Dome said, "What are all those people doing over there all packed up like they are ready to go someplace?"

Helen said, "They are waiting on the bus to take them to Houston."

"How are they going to get there with all the roads messed up and everything?" Jack said.

"They are going by boat and the Reverend Leonard is escorting them there," Helen said.

"What do you know about this preacher?" Jack asked.

"The preacher said he was kin to that very well respected Minister Bigfoot Leonard," she said.

Jack seemed a little more than a bit concerned about this trip thing to Houston. "You know Ms. Helen," Jack said, "many people have been coming down to the Dome and the Center from the beginning of the announcement of the impending disaster. Some of those people came in real need of help, some came to actually help us. But others have come with a more dubious intent. Many are selling salvation right here on the spot at a price you can't afford to pay. Others are selling shelter from the storm, cash and carry to the Astrodome. Ms. Helen," Jack said, "good sailing and we wish all of you well," as he and his friends moved on.

XXIV

DREAMS DEFERRED

Joyce said, "Folks, it looks like we're in for another hot summer day with no let-up in sight. So why don't we find a little shade from this heat."

Marge said, "Let's just go across the street. There is some shade over there, we can talk and watch the action from there. Things should be picking up soon over here, we have not seen it this quiet in awhile."

Joyce said, "Now that things have settled down somewhat, why don't we ask Ms. Helen to bring us up to date on the Nortons and the Leonards since she seems to know them quite well."

"Listen to me, Joyce," said Helen, "There is a lot I can tell you and that fine young preacher about his kin. The Nortons and the Leonards all grew up with my family back there in Gert Town. They all were a generation or two ahead of me, but I knew them well," said Helen.

Joyce said, "Helen, why don't you tell us something about the little thing you carried on with the main man. We don't think your relationship with the Bigfoot, as you called him, was purely monastic. Now do we, Mr. Smitty?"

"Joyce, don't get me into this."

Helen said, "Now you listen to me Missy, there was one I knew only too well. He was the Reverend James Henry Leonard and he was proudly penned the Bigfoot Leonard by everyone who knew him, even the children." Helen seemed to have feelings of joy and sorrow. "He was a good man, you know! Joyce, you don't know, in our day, and Mr. Smitty you can vouch for this, only a few young colored girls could dream and have any part of that dream come true. You may not know it lady, today most of us our women don't even have the luxury of a dream deferred."

Joyce said, "Helen, I'm sorry for what was said. Please forgive."

Helen said, "It must be this bitter heat."

"We still would like to hear about the Bigfoot," Joyce said, "Wouldn't we Mr. Smitty?"

Helen began.

HELEN

It was late in the afternoon on this fall day. School had been out for some time. I was on the couch doing my homework waiting for mother to come home.

They were approaching from across the street- my mother, two ladies, Mrs. Harris and Mrs. Hamilton, both of whom I know. There was this big man with them who looked like he was ten feet tall. I did not know who he was.

All four made a quick walk-through of the house and I heard them agree the large room would be suitable for the Bible group or other meetings. My mother said, "I have to talk to my husband about the group. I am sure he will be alright with it. We have had group studies before."

They set the meeting at the house for two weeks from this Thursday. For reasons that I didn't know the meeting never took place. Mother didn't explain to me why the session was postponed and she didn't have to since I was not part of the meeting. Except the Preacher sparked my interest, but he was gone.

One day, in a very casual moment I asked, "Mother, who was the man who wanted to do a Bible study here?"

She said, "He is the Reverend Bigfoot Leonard. He is very well known in New Orleans and throughout the South. It would be an honor for us to have him lead our Bible study right here in our house."

About a year later the reverend was the main speaker at the conclave in the Louisiana Avenue Baptist Convention Hall. Mother and I attended the convention and his eyes lit up. He apologized to mother for the cancellation of the study. Then and there they put together another Bible study at our house. Mother wanted the group to meet every Thursday- the regular Bible study evening. The reverend said he could only attend on the fourth Thursday of the month, because of other religious duties that prevented him from meeting every Thursday. Before mother could say anything I jumped in and said, "Mother, every fourth Thursday should be ok, if that is alright with you."

Mother paused and gave me this once-in-a-lifetime strange look and said, "Reverend, the fourth Thursday would be just fine." With the look mother gave me I knew she would say something on our way home, yet she didn't utter a word and I was glad to let it go.

Mother had received several phone calls from him that I knew nothing about. It was not until our most recent meeting that I found out about the calls. In February, as Mother and I were leaving a christening at the New Jerusalem Baptist Church, the reverend was entering to offer the introduction at the Young Adult Conference. The reverend was so happy to see us he asked if we would stay for his speech. Mother declined. I was disappointed.

Our Baptist Council of the Southern Youth had concluded on this Sunday. April showers were coming down. I was outside waiting on Mother to pick me up.

Out of nowhere the Bigfoot drove up to pick up some members. When the man laid eyes on me he could not believe what his eyes had focused on. There I was in my youth standing tall in all my glory. The man flipped out with joy and I added to his pleasure with my arms wide open and a great big smile on my face. We hugged and made arrangements to see each other before Mother arrived. Mother came, they talked, he promised to be at the next meeting, and we drove away as he waived goodbye.

The word of the meeting had been passed around to a select group of Mother's lady friends. The seating was arranged by me with four chairs and a coffee table on each side of the room. Mother had her chair to the side at the door watching for anyone who might drop by.

The Bigfoot was sitting at the head of the room. After the prayer the reverend announced the study for this evening was the Book of Ruth, the female ancestors of our Lord and Savior. Mother stated that one of her primary interests was the study of women of the Bible. The ladies were very pleased.

The study moved very well and when there was a pause Mother said, "We have coffee and some fancy appetizers," with a slight laugh. "I will introduce my loving daughter to everyone when she brings in the coffee tray."

I served the ladies, even Mother, before serving the reverend. He was sitting in a deep-seated leather armchair. I was standing in front and above him as he was getting up to complete the greeting. I said, "No Reverend, please keep your seat."

This long-legged skinny girl bending over the reverend as he gazed directly at me and I looked at him as I was dripping coffee in his coffee cup. I was wearing my light yellow cotton dress with little red hearts and tiny blue hummingbirds. The length fell just below the bend in my knee and it was worn very well. A couple of mother's dear friends looked at me in a bitter state of mind. So what? I knew my time had arrived.

They said the session went very well and thanked us for a wonderful evening as we escorted them to the door. When he was leaving, the reverend gave me an "I don't know what to do" look as he walked outside and talked with Mother. I giggled and closed the door behind him.

Mother said, "You look so beautiful in that pretty gingham dress you are wearing."

"Thank you Mother."

She said, "For such a light occasion." Mother said nothing more as she waited for Father to come home.

All of the future Bible studies went well. Mother was very happy with the group and I did my best to stay out of sight.

At first my meetings with the reverend were on and off and somewhat tight lipped. The last thing I wanted was Mother to get wind of any casual get-together with me and the reverend. Yes, on one of his shopping trips I met him downtown. He always shopped at the finer stores on Canal Street. The white sales ladies, Joyce, (there were no colored sales people in the downtown stores, except those passing for white), and the white lady shoppers, looked at me with such disgust and hatred. I didn't know what to make of it. I didn't care what they thought of me. I did not want any trouble because I did not want Mother to find out I was out with the reverend. I was glad to get out of that store.

One Saturday evening we met under the big clock at Canal and Baronne. He had finished shopping and we were greeting each other with joyous hello's. Four white ladies walked by us, turned and gazed and stared at me with such hatred. I could not believe what I was seeing. They did not say a word to me- just looked. I looked back at them. I was not going to let their hatefulness boss me around. I am my own person and stared back at them.

At some later date the reverend had to make the pastors conventions and speaking tours from Boston down to Baltimore and he would be gone for some time. He promised to get in touch as soon as he returned as he always did. "It is good you're going away for awhile because I think Mother may have gotten wind of our little get-togethers," I said. "I saw one of her friends downtown when we were talking. I didn't think she saw me but maybe she did," I said.

"Something been worrying me and I want to talk to you about it. Reverend when we are downtown why do those white ladies always gaze and stare at me with such hatred and resentment? Why do they have to hurt me? I'm just like them. They have everything. When I was a young girl I used to wonder what it is like to be white. You know, Reverend, not just to look white or like some colored people passing for white, but to really be white."

The reverend said, "I don't know for sure, but there are some things you just have to get rid of."

"Then, Reverend, why don't they get rid of their hatred?"

XXV

Urban Removal

Helen continued her story.

In the old days, Joyce, we had a large colored population in the River Bend as we used to call it. On Sundays the reverend would preach at one of the churches in the Irish Channel or in the Upper or Lower Garden District. He had a large following and on any Sunday we would pack the churches just to hear him preach. And the man gave us the Word.

As things usually go for us colored people, anyway, we got the sad news. The city was planning to place the River Bend neighborhoods in the Urban Renewal program. We all knew the St. Thomas housing project was a totally white segregated housing project. What we finally figured out was that they wanted to extend the white only policy to the entirety of the River Bend. They wanted to wipe us out from the Central City area to the Mississippi River. They wanted us out at all cost to us.

Folks, we had a fight on our hands with no help from anyone but ourselves. The reverend was in the forefront of the fight to save our great communities. We wanted a low-income housing development in the program and a stay in any immediate evacuation of low-income people from these communities. The mayor and his committees promised that all federal laws would be complied with and our concerns would be properly addressed. Our greatest mistake we took the mayor at his word. While we were still having meetings with these people, plans were underway for the actual destruction of our neighborhoods. They executed their plans so fast we did not have ample time to put in place any kind of defense that would save our communities.

The city and the government never intended to address our demands. It was the same old plan- we give and they take. In the end we discovered what we should have known in the beginning. Urban Renewal in our case means Urban Removal. Some families moved across the River and some down to the Desire Street Project. It took a little less than two years to move all the families out of our neighborhoods. The River Bend, as we used to call it, was gone forever.

The Bigfoot knew the Reverend JJ Jackson, pastor of the Mount Zion Baptist Church in the Lower 9th Ward. Reverend JJ invited us to come down and look around. He said, "We have plenty of land for sale down here. Most of my members will welcome you with open arms. That," he said, "by and large goes for the entire neighborhood. You folks gotta know everybody down here is family." Just about all of the members from our churches relocated to the Lower 9th Ward. About that same time there was a large migration of sharecroppers from the Mississippi delta region moving in to the Lower 9. Some of the locals were outraged by what they said were the criminal element from uptown and those croppers coming in from Mississippi ruining their neighborhood. What the good citizens didn't know? They were under siege. The government and St. Bernard Parish were at the same time closing down that all Black township of Fazendeville. The government forced them to move out and most of them moved to the Lower 9th Ward.

With such a mixture of different people, the long-standing residents didn't take too kindly to this mix. After several tense encounters with the locals, we all decided to talk to each other. To some extent we got some things done. After all, all we wanted was to move on and get on with our lives. The Reverend JJ and his congregation treated all of us, regardless of where we were from, as brothers and sisters and of course we are. Reverend JJ gave the Bigfoot the second and fourth Sundays of each month until he got his own church up and running again. The Bigfoot would co-pastor on those mornings with JJ.

When those two preachers put their heads together for the very first time, let me tell you Joyce, you knew the Lower 9th Ward would never be the same.

You should have seen the show these boys put on. Reverend JJ would stand in the pulpit and would start in a very low moaning voice and as it rose to a high pitch, the front door would fling wide open and the man everyone came to see would jump in. He would sashay his way up the middle of the aisle as he trembled in a steady gait on his way to the pulpit. By this time JJ had come down and they met face to face like two famous warriors shouting scripture at each other like the passages just jumped from the Bible. As the band played on there was not a seated person in the church. Every sister was shouting, stomping and screaming- you could hear them a block away. Let me tell all of you something. Mount Zion rocked.

When things quieted down a little bit, Bigfoot strolled up onto the pulpit. While all of this was going on he kept that famous toothpick in his mouth. It was a solid gold cross and when he looked out upon his people he stuck that gold cross in the lectern. Reverend JJ was already at the other end of the pulpit and they would preach the gospel to the world. Those preachers, as good as they were, no doubt in anybody's mind had received the Word from up on high. The Bigfoot performed like the *star everyone came to see. Nobody was ever disappointed. They were crying in happiness, clapping, and trying to touch him has he made his way to the vestibule in a downtown stutter's walk.*

XXVI

RETURN OF THE PREACHER MAN

By this time the passengers were boarding the buses. We got a good sideline view from across the street. Things seemed to be moving well. The reverend and his driver walked over and said, "We saw you good people over here this morning. I surmise," he said, "You folks are not making this journey with us."

"That's right."

"Well," he said, "Let me introduce myself once again. I am the Reverend Eugene Leonard Norton. Everyone knew the Reverend Leonard. He was my kin on my mother's side. She gave me his name."

Helen said, "Reverend you have a good man's shoes to fill. If you can walk in his shoes, you will be able to carry the Word any place you want to go." She said, "It's good to meet you pastor."

Reverend Norton said, "We are headed to the Jackson Street Ferry and on to the First Street Wharf. The boat for Houston will arrive there later on today." As the passengers waved goodbye we sought shelter from the sun under a mighty oak tree.

XXVII

ALL THINGS MUST END

When we sat down, Helen continued her story.

On this lovely spring day some years later I called Mother and asked if she had some time to share with me, and she said, "Yes come on over." Mother and I talked for a while about nothing in particular. At one point during our chat she looked at me. "You're not acting your usual self today. Your warmth and your usual happy face don't seem to be there today." Mother never inquired into my affairs and this day was no exception. However, out of nowhere she said, "Your father and I were married for fifty-two years and we made that promise to each other and it was never broken. Death separated us from this earth, but we will meet again in heaven to keep the promise throughout all eternity. I have no doubt that your father was a wonderful husband and a great father."

"Mama, please, tell me did he know?"

Mama said, "Your father was no dummy, yet he never breathed a word about your undertaking nor did I to him."

I said, "You probably have already guessed why I am here."

She said, with a smile, "However grown you get don't forget you are my child and I am your mother. The telephone is still in the living room."

The overpass crossed Washington Avenue just in front of the University, where I had stood many times waiting for the Bigfoot to pick me up. Here I was standing once again, but not waiting for the pickup. The sun was weak and the evening was nice with a pleasant, soft, blowing breeze in my face. I let down my hair, which he often spoke to in admiration as the breeze kept it in flight, and it fell below my shoulders. His automobile was moving south, of course, in my direction. It was a good feeling, as usual. There he stood in all his glory. The Bigfoot with that never-ending smile on his face.

"Look at you," he said, "I am glad you never cut that beautiful walnut brown hair of yours," as he always called it. We embraced.

"Reverend I have a very short statement to make. My hope is that you clearly understand what I am about to say."

He said, "I will not interfere until you tell me I can talk. But first please continue and complete your statement."

"Thank you. Reverend, our relationship must now come to an end. We must move on with our separate lives in our own separate worlds. Reverend do you have anything to say?'

"Yes," he said, "Why don't you pause for a moment or two, then I will start. Let me say this so you will know we are both on solid ground. When you think about leaving, you are already gone. At this moment, I clearly know that. I am truly happy for you. I am happy for me. This was a truly great relationship. This is a wonderful ending to our beautiful beginning. I appreciate you more than you will ever know. You are a wonderful lady."

He put his hands on my shoulder. We hugged and he stepped back with his head to the ground. As he raised his head we made eye contact. He said, "Yellowgirl." He took another step. "I will tell you what's in my heart." He stepped away from me with eyes full of tears. He said, "You will always be my little Yellowgirl." We embraced again. "You will be with me always. I want you to know that," he said.

I walked away in painless agony. Yet I could feel the pain and strain in his heart. I drove south, he went north, as we waived each other forever goodbye.

XXVIII

The Death of JJ

Helen looked down the road where the buses had disappeared. She said, "It is good to see some of these folks get out of here and try to do some good for themselves. I used to do some traveling myself, mostly with the Bigfoot. I was kind of young when he first took me all the way up north to New York, just the two of us. Now mind you Joyce, we went many places with the other groups, but you know sometimes we had to get away to ourselves."

"Do you ever hear from anybody from the old groups? What ever happened to JJ and the Bigfoot as you would call them?" Joyce asked.

"You know Joyce," Helen said, "During Katrina they have kind of been on my mind. Them two, JJ and the Bigfoot. Yes they have. It has been a long time, but when I am thinking about them it seems like just yesterday."

HELEN

The last time I heard anything, my cousin and I had just finished helping Mother with her chores as we did whenever we were at Mother's house. The three of us were on our way to church to give praise to our loving Savior on this beautiful Sunday morning. We heard the quiet voices at the door as the sisters entered- they were two of Mother's church members. They carried the sad news on this restful spring day.

Ms. Judy, the older sister, edged to the front of her seat and spoke in a soft, quiet voice. The Reverend JJ Jackson, she said, had been summoned by the last will and testament to preach the eulogy of his dearest friend and fellow pastor the Reverend Albert Horace Winfield, minister of the Greater Bayou Baptist Church on the Bayou. Ms. Judy told us the boys spent most of their childhood in the Lower 9 and in the summer would journey to the Bayou. Both young men married the daughters of their pastors' churches. After their religious training, Reverend Winfield journeyed north to shepherd his father's flock at the church on the Bayou. JJ planted himself firmly in the Lower 9 among his family members and friends, the place of his birth.

Joyce, just for your information, JJ was a tall, lean, handsome man with a well-built frame, with slightly recessed light gray eyes, and an uncommonly pointed nose with a deep, smooth jet black complexion and a beautiful set of sparkling white teeth. The way Ms. Judy told us, JJ was not only on his way to heed the call but also to bear *witness to the devotion of their long and ever-lasting friendship and to meet, but never again, on the Bayou. JJ and his wife, matriarch of the church, mother of their three children, a lady beloved and so well respected by all, rode quietly in the passenger seat of their chauffer-driven Rolls Royce. He was so honored, yet saddened by the occasion of his pilgrimage.*

Ms. Judy told us the highway was shielded by the mighty sky-high live oak trees all were interlaced with our magnificent southern belle, the beautiful crape myrtles. It was a quiet and peaceful day of rest, the drive was easy and the road was smooth en route to the Bayou. JJ laid his head in the lap of his wife of a long and wonderful lifetime. She softly stroked his head on this autumn Sabbath day. The golden brown leaves descending to the earth, without a sound, to their final resting place, captured her imagination. From his reflections in the windows she could see the brilliance fading from his eyes as the tears slowly trickled down her cheeks. The steeple of the church was in clear view as it ascended into the sky and singing could be heard as they entered onto the bayou road of the church. She clinched his hand as the tears began to flow. JJ, without a whisper, eased his way into the Promised Land on the Bayou.

XXIX

THE DEATH OF BIG FOOT

Helen continued.

*Years ago, some time after JJ's death, I was invited
to a repast in Gert Town of an old friend of the family. My
arrival was well received by the family members, but
raised eyebrows of more than a few of the older
grandmothers. I was making friendly talk with family
and some other people when the conversation got around
to me. I told them I raised a fine family- two daughters
and a wonderful son and I am the proud grandmother of
five. My husband, I said, passed on some years ago.*

*Shirley, a friend of my family, leaned over and
whispered so that only a few could hear if any,
"Girlfriend," she said, "Don't you want to know about
him?"*

I said, "Him?"

"Yes, him the Bigfoot," Shirley said.

*With a smile on my face I said, "Yes, let's take a seat
over here. After I got married I lost all contact with the
Bigfoot and our Sunday morning churchgoing friends."*

Mrs. Edna, if I recall her name correctly, one of the older grandmothers, came over and said, "You are Helen Baptiste."

"Yes, my married name is Lacour, I am Helen Lacour."

"Some years ago I heard that, but you were Helen Baptiste before."

"Yes, before I got married."

"I am Mrs. Edna Joseph DeVoe of the New Jerusalem Baptist Church. Just in case you don't remember. Back in those days there was talk in our church that you and the reverend had a little something going for quite some time. Everybody in the neighborhood knew about it. He passed over many wholesome girls in our church much older than you. All of whom were much more suited to a man of his maturity. Maybe you thought, as a few in our church did, it was the spirit which moved him to consort with the innocence of your youth."

I said to Mrs. DeVoe, "I don't know if I was chosen by him or by the spirit, or if he was chosen by me. But one thing which has always been with me is what my mama told me when I was a young girl. Mama said to me, 'Take this to the grave with you girl, it takes a good man to make a woman out of a girl. Choose wisely. You are my only child," Mama said, "and you will have a truly wonderful life."

As she walked across the room Mrs. DeVoe turned and looked straight at me and said, "I hope you don't think I have not had a truly wonderful marriage!"

"Helen!" Shirley uttered. "Don't get sidetracked by that old biddy. Look," Shirley said, "We asked the family what happened to the Bigfoot and I can tell you his family has to this day been very hush hush about the death of the man. The only thing we could get out of them was that because of his advanced age his passing was quiet and peaceful.

"But here is the word which came down to us at our church," Shirley continued, "His doctor told him to slow down, take it easy. 'At your age,' he said, 'the heart can't bear the pain it's been harboring nor the strain of time. You have lived a long and glorious life. It is time for old gents like you and me to bring our work to a close. We have nothing more to prove, we have given this life our very best. You know as well as I do your retirement age has long since passed.' The Bigfoot as we both know," Shirley said, "had too much fire in his soul for anyone to tell him to retire or slow down. His family did not tell us the whole story. When the truth was known, Helen, here is what we found out."

Shirley said, "The Bigfoot with a congregation of worshippers and faithful followers made the grand march and gathered down at the river on this blistering Sunday afternoon for a baptism of the faithful. The Bigfoot was standing on the levee of the Mississippi where the river meets the sea with his arms reaching for the sky as he walked against the tide. The Preacher said to his tried and true devoted followers, 'Brothers and sisters, as you no doubt know by now, my heart has gotten weaker and weaker and my health is failing, as he moved deeper and deeper against the tide. My road to our magnificent and worthy place in the heavens has grown shorter and shorter. Time has passed me by,' he said as he walked farther and farther against the oncoming tide.

"Out of this turbulent sea rose a gigantic tidal wave. It was as high as the heavens, the likes of which had never been witnessed before," Shirley uttered. "The faithfuls said it was the hand of the almighty which gently scooped up the Bigfoot as he reached for the heavens. His believers of unshakeable faith were praying, shouting, clapping and screaming. We were told the members were singing, 'The Bigfoot done made his way to the Promised Land! The rapture is at hand.'"

I said, "That's my Bigfoot. He had to go out with a bang. The man had just too much fire in his soul."

"Girlfriend," Shirley said, "Have you had a wonderful life?"

I said, "What do you think? Shirley, it is time for me to go," and moved on.

That was a different day. It was tough for us just to hold on in my day. Change was hard to come by. We were treated less than human as some of you may know. In our day we were sent men like the Reverends JJ and the Bigfoot Leonard to guide us through those hard times. They were not perfect. Most were flawed. But they were ours, they were homegrown. We all tried to move our people to a better place. We did. From what I can see here of late, our leaders are junior partners of the oppressors. We are a voiceless people. What happened to the men who shouldered our burden for a better life for our women and children? It is not meant for the women to carry the burden of life alone. The way of the man is the way of the woman.

XXX

THE MARCHERS

As we tried to escape the heat on this merciless hot summer day, some people were forming groups. Isaac, a person I knew, beckoned us to come over. My friend said, "Smitty used to work in the labor movement in Chicago." He said, "We tried to march for food and stuff but our march did not work out too well. We would like you to help us put this thing together if you can."

I said, "There is no use of marching on City Hall or trying to talk to our Mr. Mayor. If he lowers himself to greet us we will not get anything but B.S."

Frank said, "Let's go to the Dome and protest our demands directly to the military people. They seem to be in charge of everything. Now if we can just get organized."

Linda said, "Let's get it together and start marching. We are not doing ourselves any good standing out here in this heat."

Tony said, "Do we know if the military is still at the Dome?"

"We saw some military people and some FEMA people who looked like they were in charge. They were giving out orders," Earl said.

"Let's march on then," Ken said. "They didn't even know we are over here. How's about that? We know we are over here and with the march the whole world will know we are over here. What we have to drive home to them is that there are thousands, and we mean thousands, of people over here at the Center. They gotta get over here and straighten this place out before holy hell breaks loose. Our people need food and medical attention and everything. Some people have not had any food since the army ran out of food a couple days ago. We need help now. Another thing we have to make them understand in no uncertain terms- most of us are not leaving New Orleans regardless of what their orders are."

Many of the people said, "We are down with that."

Isaac, the leader, said, "We got to have about five hundred people or more if we want to kick this off right."

Earl said, "Looks like we have many more than that now, we should pick up more people on the way. That number will make an impression on them. We want our demands met."

Isaac said, "Let's get to marching. Smitty see you later- we are out of here!"

Helen said, "It looks like they are going to get things done."

Joyce said, "I am sure they will. Smitty," she said, "do you have any little thing to add?"

"Yes," I said. "They have a well organized group. They know what they need to do and they are gonna get things done."

Joyce said, "Thank you, Mister Smitty," as our group moved closer to the Center. In spite of the glaring heat, our group strolled, waving and talking to many people. There were so many people who had very serious problems we just could not listen to all of them. No doubt some of them were critically in need of medical attention. We noticed the conditions in the Center had so deteriorated that people were saying this situation was brought on by the designed neglect of our government. The people were neglected beyond shame.

James expressed to our group, "If there were ten thousand to fifteen thousand white people living under these conditions the government would be there in a moment with all the assets at its disposal."

XXXI

RETURN OF THE BOAT PEOPLE

On our way back to the Center we ran into a disappointed group of boat people. We finally calmed them down. Their leader, Nelson, said, "The preacher man ripped us off!"

James said, "Tell us what happened after you left here this morning?"

Nelson told us.

NELSON

We left here and went down to the water. We gathered at the river and gave praise to the Almighty for sending us the reverend and for a safe and wonderful journey into the unknown. The reverend led us in prayer. We started our journey from the Jackson ferry- we were singing and making merry. It was a beautiful short walk to the Wharf. The Preacher said the buses had to go and pick up the passengers at the Dome. We all understood that. At the wharf the Preacher went in and made the final arrangements. So he said. He came back and said the ship would be here in one hour or less.

The Preacher said, "Please bear with the heat, in a short time we will be on our way."

"Will you be with us?" Phylis asked.

The preacher said, "Not this time. The Lord is keeping me behind to complete his work."

We said we understood. An hour and a half had passed and everybody was getting upset. I said to them, "Let me go inside and see what is going on."

The place looked abandoned except for the night clerk. He said, "These wharves been closed since Saturday. There will not be another ship docking at these wharfs until after the emergency closing order is lifted. That probably won't be until next week sometime at best." There was nothing I could say to the people. When I got outside I just started screaming and they all started crying. I didn't have to tell them anything. They all knew what had happened.

On our way over here to the Center we ran into Wesley and his group from the Dome who also were looking for the so-called preacher and his people. Wesley and his group wanted to know our situation. We told them the game the preacher played and how he had ripped us off. He never intended to take us to Houston or anyplace else. After we heard their painful story, Wesley *wanted us to join in the hunt for the preacher man and his boys. Wesley and his boys had all kinds of guns and knives and whatever. Wesley said, "When we find them we are going to kill them pure and simple. They had no right to take our money like that. When we find them we are gonna get em and get them good. They won't rob anybody else. We guarantee you that."*

Wesley said, "Many of these old people gave up some of the last money they had. The sad part about the whole thing- so many said they thought the preacher man was sent by the Almighty to take us to dry land. You have never seen so many heartbroken people when we all found out the preacher man was an angel of the devil."

Horace, an older person in our group, told them, "Folks, you have lost your money. Give up this search. The money ain't coming back. Now live with it."

"Man, you are talking about our $5,000 and ain't no telling what these other people lost! And you want us to just give it up and quit just like that?" Wesley said.

When Nelson finished his story, Irene said, "Maybe we should go to the police."

"What police?" Ben said. "Who knows? They may be in on the cut. I noticed yesterday the Cadillac and buses had out-of-state plates. Give it up people. They are gone and your money is gone. They are both gone."

XXXII

CHILDREN OF THE CENTER

Jimmy said, "Folks don't you think it's time we get on back to the group, and check on the fellows guarding our stuff? We don't want anybody tampering with our hard-earned begotten goods. You know?"

As we got close to the group, Helen said, "Mr. Smitty, look what's waiting for you."

I said, "What?"

She said, "Look y'all, the man has a fan club."

I said, "Miss Helen give me a break, I am burned out!"

Joyce said, "Looks like the boys and their mother are waiting on you so perk it up and get your talking self together."

Jimmy said, "Well we are back at the old homestead. Might as well plot ourselves down here. Everything looks good to me."

Ms. Lakendra, the boys' mother, said, "They have been talking about you all morning. I said to them, 'Mr. Smitty just might have gone.' Little Ray said, 'No he ain't.

He promised he would talk to us but it was too late last night.'"

I said, "Miss, I am willing to talk to the boys, but I need a few minutes or so to get myself together."

Joyce said, "Give the man some time. He ain't going nowhere." People were coming and going in our group. I wondered if I could get in a little space up against the wall inside the Center. Before I got too deep inside I noticed the place was too crazy for me, so back outside to the group.

Ray said, "Mama, look, Mr. Smitty is coming back."

I said to the boy, "Let me get myself settled in son, and you can ask me any questions you wish." The group seemed to have expanded to about fifty or so noisy people. As I was stepping over and around bodies trying to get a seat, little Ray looked up and said, "Mr. Smitty, you are old. Did you live in the slavery times?"

I shot back with a fast, loud, "No! I am old, but not that old." The crowd got a little giggle out of that and settled down.

Sean said, "Mr. Smitty, last night you told us you would tell us about the times we were in slavery. You said you would tell us like the old folks used to tell you kids when you were our age."

"Mr. Smitty," Brad said, "We don't know any old people who would talk to us about things like that."

I began: "Longtime ago when our history was explained to us and our dreams were talked about, many of our old folks, like my Uncle Billy and Cousin Beatrice, used to gather and the young like you would listen to our relatives talk about slavery and freedom. Cousin Beatrice, most people called her Bea for short, told us slavery and freedom were always on their minds, and those were the never-ending topics of conversations. Uncle Billy Jefferson took the lead at most of those meetings with other likeminded older people. The man said he was born in 1864, some said not until the 1870s, the family said we don't quite know and it really doesn't matter.

"Mister Sam Angelino and his family lived upstairs over the grocery bar which they owned at Andry and Urquhart in this just about all Black neighborhood. Cousin Bea was the barkeep. Almost every Sunday, Uncle Billy, not a man of faith by any means, with his church-slacken family members and friends, would walk the block, pick up what they needed for the moment from the bar, and head across Andry Street. Most of the men were sitting in a broken circle on large old milk crates perched on patches of unkempt St. Augustine under this magnificent, mighty oak tree. Its branches almost reaching the clouds in every direction, forming a shady umbrella from the sun and a great stage to beat their gums. The children came to listen and see the show.

"For these old gents it was just as much about looking good as it was about how we have been treated from the first day we set foot on this land. And they went at it just about every Sunday. However the crowd grew larger and more enraged and things went into high gear on those Sundays when word came down that our all-white police force had beaten some poor Negro within inches of his life, or had killed a Black man in their custody that Saturday night in plain execution style. Some of the young adults in their twenties and twenties did the beer thing, but as I can remember there was very little hard liquor. Some of the men were on their knees shooting craps and others were standing around betting pennies and nickels until the police showed up. Sometimes the players would scoff what little coins were there and walk away. Other times the police would say to the kids, "Go get the change, y'all can have what's there."

"The odd thing about all the dice players— they would not let the kids watch the games. They would always run the kids away and the kids knew better than to play around the games. They would always say, 'You kids came here to listen to the old heads, so get over there.'

"This Sunday was not unlike most others. Things were getting underway. The people were waiting for Uncle Billy to come up the street to get things going. The crowd was somewhat taken back when they saw Uncle Billy and his older brother, the Reverend Thomas Joseph Jefferson, with several of his members walking in our direction. It was not expected that the reverend or any of his members would ever be present at any of these gatherings. After all the reverend had his church and a flock to shepherd.

"Reverend Thomas seemed to have gotten some kind of okay but Uncle Billy did not appear to be in total agreement with whatever the deal was. As Reverend Thomas walked into the center of the crowd, the mood changed and the people did not seem too happy. This looked like it was going to be some kind of sermon or some preachy thing like that. And that was not what these people came to hear. The reverend in the center was flanked by his members. Uncle Billy was on the sidelines with his arms folded and the Reverend Thomas took charge of the coming together and took the people in a different direction this Sunday.

XXXIII

BROTHER AGAINST BROTHER

Rev. Thomas: Dear brothers and sisters. All of your talks heretofore have been about slavery-slavery and more slavery. That endless chatter has gotten you no place. Good people, slavery is over and we have to put it to rest if progress is to be made. I came here this Sabbath day to ask that we bury that sad chapter in our history in the graveyards of evil. We got to move on and I am asking you to carry on with me this new quest for freedom.

Uncle Billy: Can you believe what my brother just asked you to do? He asked us to forget about slavery. No we can't and we will not let those who put us in slavery forget about it either. Now listen people, and to you the young, the institution of slavery was a criminal enterprise. The people who created that penal enterprise, and their offsprings who no doubt benefitted from it, are without a doubt criminal. No one can deny.

Rev. Thomas: I know slavery is against the laws of scripture. Some day we know the masters will have to pay their just due to us and the Almighty. As you folks can see I am not trying to excuse the masters for their evil deeds or anything else they did to us. But to keep beating the rock of slavery is a waste of your precious time and mine.

Uncle Billy: People, listen to me. To forget about slavery, as my brother has asked, is to forget about ourselves. We all know slavery, like no other event in the history of America, makes us who we are. Our history, would you believe, would never let us forget about slavery.

Rev. Thomas: Our enemy is not what is dead and buried but that which is in the way of our complete and unfettered freedom. To be a full citizen we must have those freedoms, and we are going to get them. We cannot stand in our own way. We have to move forward. When this is all over we are going to get our freedom and in the end we are going to be just as free as the white man.

Uncle Billy: Folks, did you hear what the man said? Let me repeat this. Our Uncle Tom said in the end we gonna be free just like the white man. I say whoopeedo! If we look at what the brother is saying we ain't never ever going to be free. Everyone knows that in the white man's mind this is a country without end. The white man did not do the African thing and the slavery thing to now set us free. If the master wanted to free up anybody it would have been the Indian. Right. Just look what he did to them.

Rev. Thomas: The Indian placed his faith in the tools of war to make peace with the masters. War was the wrong way to achieve peace. What history teaches is that we should use the power of the great Negotiator, which never fails, and let the Master make peace with our Creator.

Uncle Billy: He came to this Indian land, got all the help he wanted from them, and as soon as he got a foothold, whammo! He killed off as many Indians as he could get his hands on in daylight or darkness. What few were left he rounded up, forced them into detention camps. The white man became the new owner of the Indian land. The Indians became refugees in these detention camps without ever having the right of coming back to their ancestral lands.

Rev. Thomas: I will be the first to say that situation between those good peoples got out of hand after such a great beginning. Both groups, I would say, should have extended an open handed policy to each other instead of resorting to the destructive tools of war. Let me say this, I don't think the primary aim of the Master was to put the Indian in slavery or bondage.

Uncle Billy: When you look at it, the Indian is in bondage in the land of his ancestors and will never again be as free as he once was and will never be as free as the white man. The white man gave the Indian a brand new white man's name- the Native American. Why my brother doesn't get the message that the man never intended for us to be free? From day one he wanted us to be in bondage to him forever. And that's the reason behind all these segregation laws.

Rev. Thomas: Friends, the very first thing we have to get settled is that this whole matter is beyond our human control. We can get the justice and freedom so promised us if we pursue our goals through moral persuasion and divine intervention only. Victory will not come to us through political activism, as my brother wants. Let me tell you the way of my brother is the wrong way. Political activism will fail you- mark the words of this man of faith.

Uncle Billy: Children, I don't want to question my brother's faith or yours not one bit. But we don't have one drop of real proof that moral persuasion or divine intervention helped in any way to get us off the plantation. A few do believe, if left to the Great Persuader, we would still have chains around our ankles and whips about our backs!

Rev. Thomas: As a pastor to the gospel and a shepherd to the poor and young, let me tell you I am not trying to forgive those awful masters for any of their transgressions they committed in the past. We no longer have chains around our ankles, and as everyone can see, we are not saying we are anywhere near full freedom, but things have changed for the better as all bear witness to the facts.

Uncle Billy: What's with all this righteousness and broken chain business and all of that other stuff my brother's trying to peddle to all of you? Remember, here of late the preacher and his friends have been preaching that we are the New Negro, whatever that means. Let me warn you people and you kids also to be aware of the clever peddlers. They will not tell you what they are selling. Are they selling real freedom or peddling just another kind of bondage?

Rev. Thomas: We too must change if we are going to move forward in attaining our goals. As we all know, it is right and just to forgive even our harshest transgressors. We cannot defeat this horrible system of segregation ourselves. I can assure my little brother and all of you doubters, it was the intervention of the Almighty that broke the

links forever that bound us to those dreadful times.
We are on the march.

Uncle Billy: I can tell you, the links my brother
speaks of, to this day have not been broken. Look
children, if we are going to be free here is what I
think. You can break the links that binds his ankles,
you can remove him from the plantation and you
can even tell him he is free to go. But until he
unshackles the chains of slavery from around his
mind he will be in bondage all the days he creeps
upon the earth. The way things are going for us,
who in the hell knows, we all just might wind up
slaves in the Great Beyond. Wouldn't that be
just great!

XXXIV

RAPE OF THE SLAVE GIRL

The children were listening attentively. Brad asked, "Mister Smitty, do you think we will ever be free like white people?"

I smiled and continued. "Let me tell you another story. It was a mild morning. People were coming and going. Business at the bar was better than usual for a Sunday morning. Uncle Billy and the boys had picked up their goodies and their regular ritual was in full swing under that mighty oak tree across the street, where women were seldom seen and never heard.

"Before noon a family friend, Miss Pauleen, gave my Cousin Bea a message from my great aunt Martha. Cousin Bea told her boss Mister Angelino she had been called to the bedside of Aunt Martha, and Mike would take over for her. Miss Pauleen said, 'Aunt Martha regrets she is unable to rise today. Please bring the children- she would be pleased to see them.'

"Bea said, 'Come on children, we don't want to take all day getting there. There is a lot we can learn from Aunt Martha, after all, she is the oldest member of our family.'

"We arrived at Aunt Martha's house. 'Good afternoon Aunt Martha,' Cousin Bea said. 'I see you are talking to some of our children. I brought some of these young girls and boys to see you.'

"'I see you did,' she said. 'How are you girls and boys today?'

"Cousin Bea said, 'We heard that the Doctor was at your bedside during the middle of the week.'

"'Yes, Bea,' Aunt Martha said, 'Dr. Dejon was here a morning or two ago. He asked me, "How are you feeling?"

"' "You know, Doctor, here of late I have not been feeling too well. Even for an old lady, I thought when the doctor came in the morning I would be feeling a little bit better. But Doctor I don't feel that good at all."

"' "Aunt Martha," the Doctor said, "You are not alone in that feeling. When I woke up this morning I didn't feel too good myself. I know all of us old folks would like to get well. But Sister Martha let me tell you, your condition has not changed for the better since my last visit two weeks ago Wednesday."

"'I said, "Doctor, if my condition is staying just about the same, maybe I am getting a little bit better after all."

"' "No, Sister," he said. "It doesn't work that way."

"' "What I am trying to get at Doctor," I said, "I would like to meet my maker feeling a little bit better, Sir, even though I know I will never get well. Isn't it your job to make me feel a little bit better, Doctor? So please do your duty."

"'He left a little tiffed, but he will be back, he is my doctor,' she said.

"Cousin Bea said, 'Aunt Martha, it would be nice if these young people could hear some of those things you suffered during those dark days of slavery and on.'

"'Bea, dear girl,' she said, 'those days have not gone away. We are just in a different kind of darkness. But I don't want to jump ahead of myself.'

Aunt Martha began:

AUNT MARTHA

The last time I ran away I wanted to make my 17th birthday in freedom's land. But I met a couple who looked like man and wife and who told me they could help me get across the state line where there were underground camps. At the camps people would help me and the others get to freedom. The man said they knew the way since they had helped many of the runaways get to the camps before.

At the plantation everyone knew if you are going to run away first find the North Star and walk north to the star and you will reach the state line. With these two it looked like we were walking away from the star in some other direction.

I said, "Look, we are supposed to be walking to the North Star."

They said, "If you want your freedom stay with us. We know where we are going. We have been on this road to freedom many times." I figured they must know where they are going and we kept walking.

As we walked and walked for what felt like several hours I began to have this very strange feeling about them deep down inside that things were not going right. I began to look for a way out. I said to myself, when darkness falls upon us I am leaving. I am running away. I know they can't catch me and good thing they don't have guns or any weapons. "Darkness," I said to myself, "Hurry up please, you are my liberator."

Before I could get myself together there stood two white slave catchers with guns. The two slavers, as we called them back on the plantation. One said, "Get the wench over here and let's get moving." The sun had slipped beyond the horizon and the daylight had been consumed by the darkness. Sometime later we walked into this well guarded slave holding camp. The fire lit up a good deal of the people. Four white slave catchers with guns, and as far as I could tell about fifteen or so captured runaways. Both men and women were in some kind of handcuffs and were bound to each other with chains around their ankles. Everything seemed quiet and peaceful until they saw the man and woman. The runaways began to whisper in a low and repeated chant:

Snitcher, snitcher, you sold us away

Snitcher, snitcher, comes freedom day

Snitcher, snitcher, you gotta pay

The four slave catchers with their guns pointed at the runaways said, "Shut up!" with the harshest kind of words. My ankles were bound in chains like the others, but they left my hands free. I was kept separate and away from the other runaways. I laid my head back against the stump trying to get some relief from the dreadfulness of what was to come when I was returned to the plantation. Yet the brightness of the moon gave some light of hope as it pierced the darkness of the night. My mind drifted back to the plantation and I could feel the hardness of the punishment the Master had in store for me. I can't stay on the plantation, I thought. I ran away once before and I will run away again. No one can keep me from my freedom. The master gotta kill me to keep me in bondage. Oh Lord, I am so tired of being shackled to that whipping post.

The snitchers who claimed to be helping us escape to freedom stood in a huddle with the two white slave catchers and they all looked like they were in some kind of agreement talking and nodding at each other. The snitchers hurried by, dashed into the woods out of site of everyone. The more I looked at them I could not believe these snitchers were colored people just like me. They were not liberators as they claimed to be. I didn't understand how they could do what they were doing. These colored people were slave catchers pure and simple, selling out to their own kind.

They next morning just before the break of day we heard the hoof beats of several horses headed our way. Three white men on horseback told the slave catchers the news was that Lincoln had freed the slaves. "Every one of your slaves is now free to go." He said, "The master don't have any more money to pay you catchers anyway. By *now you guys ought to know their masters don't have any more federal money and if you got paid in Confederate money it ain't worth the paper it is printed on."*

One said, "I hope you guys ain't holding any Confederate paper. The masters can't keep them on the land anyway."

Master Brogan, the head slave catcher said, "We heard some time ago that this freedom thing would not be too long coming." The men on horseback rode on into the morning. Master Brogan said, "Take the cuffs off and unchain them. Let them go."

All the runaways were shouting and screaming. I gave praise the best way I knew how for this great day. I was a free woman, but I was still ankle bound. Some of the runaways fell to their knees and prayed for a while. The freed people would not leave, they were standing around as they didn't know what to do or where to go. They were mumbling to themselves and others talking to each other. The freed people were in total disbelief that this long awaited freedom day had been delivered to them as promised. One of them said, "We all know that the hand of the Lord is at work here."

The slave catcher told them they were free to go. Master Brogan told the four white guards to head on back to the camp. "And when I get back," he said, "I will settle up things."

It was so very strange. All the freed people went over and thanked the two slave catchers for their freedom. And they came over and said, "Goodbye," and, "God bless this child." Some walked away. Several ran with joy into the woods. Others went their separate ways but a few did turn and look at me sitting on a stump with my ankles bound while Master Brogan and the other slave catcher broke camp.

We had walked for several hours, it seemed like, when the slave catcher looked around and walked over to a small patch of grass. Master Brogan began stamping the grass to the ground and threw some kind of blanket on the grass. The slave catcher looked at his partner, Mr. Kelly, and said, "This is as good a place as any." Master Brogan said, "Get up wench and get on this blanket."

I said, "No."

Master Brogan said, "Did you hear that bitch say no to me? If you don't get over here now I will kill you right where you are. You ain't worth nothing to us any more. Dead or alive you ain't worth shit to me."

I said, "President Lincoln set us free. You gotta take these ankle braces off of me and let me go. I am a free woman now. You ain't my master no more."

"Wench, you ain't free until I say you are free. I am your goddamn master until the day you die!" Master Brogan said, "All our troubles started when that long legged son of a bitch up there in Washington let all these Black bastards go free." Mr. Kelly grabbed me by the arm and dragged me and flung me onto the blanket. I was too weak from the long hours of walking and lack of food. I fought them the best I could but my resistance was too low and they were two big men. Both of them did everything and anything they wanted to do to me. No matter how much I screamed and begged for mercy they would not turn me loose. I don't know how long this went on.

After they got through with me Master Brogan said, "I'm going to kill the bitch. She had the goddamn nerve to insult me, a white man. Can you believe that?" he said.

The partner said, "Let's get the hell out of here. We got what we wanted so let's just go."

I was a prisoner of the hurt and pain they caused me to suffer. Yet as I was struggling to ease the suffering, I got a brief glimpse into the face of my captor. Master Brogan seemed totally consumed by some terrible affliction which would not set him free.

Master Brogan was shouting when he said, "This bitch disrespected me and she insulted you and you just going to let her walk away? No way!"

I knew Master Brogan cannot live with such an insult and let me live. When I begged for mercy I was not begging for myself but I wanted to keep my precious womanhood, which they ravished, from me without a thought.

Mr. Kelly said, "Somebody could hear the gun shots. A Union patrol with Black soldiers could be through here any time and that could mean real trouble for us."

"Not only that," said Mr. Kelly, "If we kill her we have to bury her."

"No we don't," said Master Brogan. "Just leave the wench where she falls." I knew my captor wanted me dead but I had not resigned myself to die.

Mr. Kelly said, "We can't kill her without burying her body. That's all I have to say."

Master Brogan said, "Why in hell do we have to bury the body?"

Mr. Kelly said, "It's the Christian way."

When I finished relating the story of Aunt Martha, I said to the children. "It would be nice if they were here today, Uncle Billy, Cousin Bea and Aunt Martha, so you could get this information about slavery and freedom firsthand. Unfortunately all three have long since passed on."

I turned to their mother, "It's time these kids got to bed. I don't know about the rest of you guys, but it's time for me to move on."

On distant shores and wanting places.

Ever, to return to the land of our birth.

That precious land, that good earth.

However slow the pace, however long the walk,

We will maintain the gait.

Where our ancestors dwell in peace.

We will return to New Orleans,

That place of our birth.

-Isaac at the Windsor Ward, 2005

Day 7: Saturday, September 3, 2005

THE ENDLESS JOURNEY

35. Rastafarians Defy the Military

36. The Community-Based Group

37. Our Shattered Dreams

38. The Lost Brother

39. The Endless Journey

XXXV

RASTAFARIANS DEFY THE MILITARY

On Saturday morning we saw six or seven trucks pull across the street from the Center. People ran over to see what these trucks were carrying. It was a Rastafarian group with truckloads of food. Since so many people had not eaten in a day or so, the trucks were a welcome sight. The Rastis said, "We have lots of food- vegetables and fruits, some can goods, and lots of water and some sandwiches. We were told there were lots of people over here but they never said you had this many over here. We don't have enough to feed everybody. We will have to come back with more stuff."

As I walked toward the group Peter, the leader, met me and said, "Looks like I know you, man."

I said, "Well I don't think so but maybe so. Who knows?" I said I used to live in Chicago where there was a large Rasti community on the southwest side.

He said, "I only went to Chi a couple times so maybe not. I don't know." We introduced ourselves.

I said, "I also lived in LA."

Peter said, "Where, man? Where did you live in LA?"

"Hollywood," I said. "I owned a couple playhouses and a few coffeehouses back during the hippie days. Several Rastis were in the theatre during those days."

Peter said, "I have lots of partners who live down by the University. I used to hang out with them. We went to Hollywood sometimes to see my man's friends in plays. I liked the action up there."

I said, "I want to thank you guys for giving out this food."

Peter said, "What the heck is wrong with these people down here? I've lived here for some time now. Everything is upside down! What's wrong with the government and the state? The city is awful- no help, no nothing. What do they expect people to do?"

As I backed away I said, "Thank you guys again."

"Okay man," he said.

I was about to turn and walk away when a military unit walked up to the Rasti leader and the lieutenant asked, "What are you people doing here?"

Peter said, "We brought some food to feed these people."

The lieutenant said in a very commanding voice, "You can't feed these people." The crowds were dumbfounded. After seeing other things that were similar I was a little put out but not shocked.

Peter said, "What do you mean we can't feed the people?"

The lieutenant said emphatically, "Those are my orders. You can't give away any food."

The crowds were upset and on the verge of doing anything. The Rasti group and about seven or so of the people walked over and I asked, "What is the problem?"

Peter said, "We don't know, but will you help us talk to these people?"

"Yes, I will help. We have to first figure out what we want to do and stick with that. We all have to agree on who will be our spokesperson and stick by that person."

Peter said, "Why don't you speak for everybody?"

"Okay, I will do the talking. What is it we want to do?"

Peter said, "We want to feed the people!"

I said, "That's not enough. We have to make it clear to the military man we are going to feed our children, our brothers and sisters and our elders regardless of what the lieutenant does." I asked, "Can all of us agree on this and stick together on it?" Everyone agreed.

We walked over and before I could say anything the lieutenant said, "The city of New Orleans is under martial law and I have my orders. All of you are in violation of the law. I can arrest everyone here." Some people were having severe problems with what he was demanding. They started taking food off of some of the trucks. Some of the people got things stabilized before anything got out of control.

"Lieutenant," I said in a polite, firm voice. "Just think of the national implications of what you are doing. On the international scale, what do you think America will hear when the world learns that the U.S. Military stopped ten thousand Black Katrina victims from getting their own food? What a humanitarian disaster this will become."

The lieutenant said, "This will require a meeting with the officer in charge. We will return." The lieutenant did an about-face, marched about a quarter of the block, made a right turn, and disappeared beyond sight. Peter and the other Rastis started giving out the food as soon as the unit left. About fifteen minutes after, the military unit returned and without explanation the lieutenants stated the Rastafarians could distribute food at any time. The people were shouting and screaming with joy.

Once again, the military man did an about-face, marched about a quarter of a block away, made a right turn, and disappeared in the blinding midday sun.

XXXVI

The Community Based Group

Shortly after noon we heard the sounds of a helicopter coming in for a landing. Captain Parnell, the officer in charge, said the military had orders to evacuate the Center as soon as possible. The officer said the mission should be done in the next few days to a week. "We will eventually get everybody to the airport. We are not allowed to evacuate anyone out of here at night because we have come under too much gunfire. We can't put the citizens at risk. We will fly for a few hours during the daylight. We need to get this organized in an orderly fashion so we can move as many as possible during the small window of opportunity open to us. All of this may be an additional hardship on you but we will get everyone on board as soon as possible."

The captain said, "We will always have two lines for this operation. The line to your right will be for the sick, women with children, and the elders. They will be the first we take out. Then we will take out the rest of you. This procedure will be followed until the evacuation is complete. The evacuation will start at 3:00 PM upon our return."

They returned at 3:00 PM. The lines were ready and the officer said, "Let's get the evacuation started." The captain said, "We can only take thirteen people per trip not counting our crew. We will have many other forms of transportation as soon as they are available. You will be allowed to carry only one bag and nothing else. If you have more than one carry-on you will not be allowed to get in the helicopter. You can always wait for the available ground transportation. I don't know what their policy is concerning carry-ons."

The copter took off and we all were happy the evacuation was underway. This process, we all knew, would take several days at best unless we could get that other transportation helping us out. Today they were only going to make seven or eight trips before they stopped for the day. I took a seat up against the fence between these two long lines. I began to wonder if we were ever going to get out of here. It was going to take days and days to get all of us out of here. How could I get out of this place and from under this heat baking sun? My energy was getting low.

Some people, most of whom I knew from different groups, came over and said, "The good news is that the big action is at the Dome. The word is that the army got trucks, and some trucks with flat beds are getting the people out. The army and those other people can roll all night."

Ken said, "They want us out of there because they don't want that many poor Black people in the mighty

Superdome. It doesn't look good for our Mr. Mayor. He doesn't give a care about the city and sure doesn't give a shit about the rest of us. The thing our loving mayor wants is for him to look good. Some of our groups are broken up and most of the people are on their way to the Dome or are already there."

Larry asked, "What happens if we have to stay here all night or a couple days? The helicopter people are saying they are gonna make seven or eight more trips and shut it down till tomorrow. We gotta get out of here- this place is getting worse than a mad house."

"Our best way out of here," Lynn said, "is at the Dome."

I said, "Who are these people giving out all this information and we have not seen any of them?"

Lynn answered, "Just before we came here we were on the other street and this group came over and was telling us . . ."

Before Lynn finished someone jumped in and said, "Hold on- some of them are coming over here."

Their leader approached us and said, "My name is Karen. We are a community-based group working out of the Lower 9 that came together just after the storm when we learned the army was breaking up families and sending these broken families all over the country. We knew something was wrong. We began advising families to tell the army they wanted their families to stay together. In our meeting with the army, FEMA and others we made it clear that their own procedure did not allow them to break up the family and send members to all parts of the country. They have to, under their rules, make every effort to keep the family together. If not, the army is imposing an undue hardship on the families."

Karen continued, "We are also telling the families to tell the carriers to send them first to Baton Rouge, Texas, Mississippi and Arkansas as much as possible. These places are closest to New Orleans. We are making it clear to the authorities that so many of these people don't have the necessary resources to return home if sent too far away.

"You see," Karen said, "We don't have any information from the government or any other agency that they will bring these families back home. We have no guaranteed Right of Return. We feel it is our duty to inform the people they could get stranded in some strange, far away place, and never get back home to New Orleans. They are moving people out of the Dome so fast no one knows where they are going. We feel our job is to inform the public as best we can."

I said, "What can you tell us about the evacuation plans for the Center if any?"

She said, "From what little information we have, they are going to completely evacuate the Dome first. After that the Center. With the slow pace of the helicopters it looks like most of the people will be here a couple more days. We are telling people here at the Center and in the streets if they want to get out of here fast they got to go down to the Dome. It is their best bet."

I said to the community leader, "It appears to me that you have a good plan and are doing some very good work. I would like to thank you and your group as well. It looks like we will need all the help we can get and a lot more." Many people embraced and expressed their thanks as the community people went about their task.

I told our group, "The Dome is the fastest way out of here and I think it is the smart move you are making and I do indeed wish each of you well. However I think the best thing for me to do is to hang here and see what happens." Everyone seemed a bit stunned by my words and I was somewhat taken back by their reactions. I quickly said, "Just think, we have had some strange moments hanging on to all that water and toilet paper. Our main stay." We definitely hugged each other with a binding sadness and yet with happy smiles on our faces.

As the group began to walk away Sharon, who never had too much conversation with anyone, looked back at me and said with a smile on her face, "Toilet paper."

"Yes, toilet paper." The group moved on.

XXXVII

Our Shattered Dreams

One of the soldiers guarding the place walked over and said, "It looks like you people are pretty well burned out. You know we are doing the best we can. We are moving people from all over the city to the airport."

I said, "That's no doubt true, but I would like to get out of here."

He said, "Looks like you were one of the people at the big food giveaway a couple days ago."

"Yes, I was there. You guys gave out a few meals. You ran out of food and closed the place down and got the heck out of there fast."

"Our officer told us we didn't want any altercations with the citizens. He told us to close down and get the hell out of there."

When the helicopter landed the guard went over and talked with the officer in charge. The guard called me inside the gate. "Stay over there behind those boxes," he said. I did. Several copters landed many more times. At one point he came over and said, "You can only take one bag with you." I took my blanket from the large bag and stuffed the backpack into the bag. I took my blanket, which

I had carried, from the Lower 9 to my cousin's house, to the streets of New Orleans and to the Convention Center. Now we must part forever. I neatly folded the blanket and carefully placed it under one of the boxes. I walked away somewhat dismayed as the helicopter came and took me away.

As I looked down from the air I said, "Farewell dear blanket, farewell."

We were on the move again. The pilot said, "The flight to the airport will only take a few minutes. Hold on to your things. When we touch down we want to get everyone off as quickly as possible. We need to make as many trips as the daylight will allow." He also said, "Take a good look at the city, it may be some time before some of you see it again." There wasn't much to see beyond this vast devastation, I thought, except the city was covered under a blanket of dirty white water. It appears the rebuilding process may well exceed all expectations. New Orleans will need many people with great dreams and big ideas.

The pilot said, "Welcome to the International Airport. You will exit to your left straight ahead through the security checkpoint."

When we got to the airport the evacuation process was in full swing. We moved through security in record time. The flights were parting and we were scheduled for San Antonio. Several of us were engaged in chit chat. We noticed a group of six young ladies apparently giving some kind of instructions to a much older lady. As that group moved away from us the old lady seemed somewhat unsure which direction she was headed. As our conversation continued they all disappeared within the crowds. Our plane departed at the appointed hour and the pilot announced our height and destination time.

Without looking around the fellow next to me said, "If one takes a long, hard look at the city of New Orleans from high up in the sky one would feel this- the crumbling metropolis upon which all our dreams were shadows. The government will make every attempt to rebuild this city without any guaranteed expense for the free Right of Return of its displaced people. The city may recover somewhat, but New Orleans will never be the same without us."

XXXVIII

THE LOST BROTHER

We were on the move again and the pilot announced, "We will be landing soon." We had to be checked in at Kelly Air Force Base. The lines were so long it would take forever to check in.

We noticed the same six young girls and this old white lady headed in our direction. They took seats with us and joined our conversation. A few moments later the girls got up and walked away never to be seen or heard from again.

The old lady moved in closer and started talking. She said, "I need help and I don't know how to get it or if I am ever going to get my brother home." This caught the attention of everyone. Those few of us who were left in the group were surprised by these remarks.

"My name is Miss Milicent Diana Prevost." She continued, "The hospital people in New Orleans said after a series of life-threatening attacks my brother, George Joseph Prevost, was in a terminal state. I wanted to bring him back to St. Louis so I could see that he would be properly cared for. I wanted him buried in the family plot in our church's cemetery." At this point she became somewhat incoherent and she seemed kind of depressed. Lisa asked if she needed some medical attention. "No," Miss Prevost said. "Just a glass of water and I would like to take it easy for awhile."

The group was unable to follow the sequence of her conversation in any kind of detail, but everyone did their best. Miss Prevost said no to any kind of medical attention. She wanted to talk, she said, to clear things up in her head. "I just can't believe what they told me," she said.

MISS PREVOST

I got to the hotel a week ago Friday and went to the hospital on Saturday. The assistant said "This is not a good time to come," since they were in the process of securing the hospital. Their orders were, she said, to get the patients ready in case of an emergency evacuation. "Our major concerns are our patients' safety. It would be better for all of us and you too if you could come back tomorrow, Sunday." She added, "You can see all the workmen involved in securing the hospital. We don't want to put you or any of them in harm's way."

I said to her, "I came here to see my brother and to take him back home as soon as possible. I want to see my brother before I leave here today. May I speak to your supervisor or someone in charge?"

The assistant said, "I will have to find someone in charge. They are all busy, you know. It may take a few minutes."

I told her, "I will wait it out. I came here to take my brother home." She and an attendant ushered me upstairs.

The assistant said, "You can only have a few minutes with him. You can see everything up here is positioned just in case we have to make an immediate removal."

"I understand," I said. I saw my brother. He could not talk. He was very ill and sedated. Both of them stayed with me for that very short visit. Afterwards I returned to my hotel.

Mr. Brown, the hotel manager, said, "We have a church with a 10 AM Sunday morning service in the downtown area. Don't stray too far away because there are all kinds of weather reports coming out of the mayor's office about the hurricane headed our way. Stay close to us so you can hurry back to the hotel just in case we get a bad weather report."

The service was enjoyable and I felt much better. Some people at the church asked what I wanted to do. I explained to them I wanted to go back to the hotel, eat a little lunch, and later visit my brother. Some of them told me not to be venturing too far from the hotel because the mayor was going to issue a statement about the hurricane sometime today.

Instead of going back to the hotel on such a nice Sunday morning I went directly to see my brother. When I arrived at the hospital, the place was completely empty except for a guard and one staff member. The staff member said they got the mandatory evacuation orders late last night. The hospital immediately began the process of evacuating the patients. I asked where did they take my brother? The attendant said he did not have all of the details. "Here is what I can tell you. Most of the patients were transported to hospitals in parishes north of the lake. I don't have the names of patients or the hospitals they were transported too. There should be some administrative people here as soon as the emergency situations are lifted. The hurricane will probably hit us tomorrow. If so you should think of coming here no earlier than Tuesday, I would say."

I said to the attendant, "You sure you don't know where they took my brother?"

The attendant said, "Lady, I told you all I know."

When I got back to the hotel I said to the hotel manager, "It is good the hospital has moved my brother out of harm's way. I will thank them for their help when I go down there tomorrow."

The manager said, "The mayor has ordered a mandatory evacuation citywide. The authorities seem certain," he said, "the hurricane will hit the city early Monday morning about 6:30 AM. My advice to you," he said, "stay here tomorrow until we get the all clear signal that the danger is over."

On Tuesday I went to the hospital. The place was partially under water. The attendant said I would have to come back Wednesday and it would be better if I came in the afternoon. By that time more of the water would have drained out. I went back to the hospital on Wednesday and talked to a different staff person. She told me all of the patients' records were destroyed by the hurricane. "I have no way of knowing which hospital each of our patients is in. Until we get a report from the various hospitals we will not know who is where." I told her that I knew my brother was in this hospital and the hospital has to account for his whereabouts. She responded, "As of now we have no records. So Miss," she said, "we don't know if your brother was ever in this hospital or not." She said,

"The remainder of us have to evacuate the place because the authorities have determined the hospital to be unsafe. We hope to have temporary quarters soon. And at that time we will post the new address and contact information. That should be completed within the next several days to a week."

On Wednesday the hotel manager Mr. Brown called us together and made an announcement that the hotel had to be evacuated by noon the next day, Thursday. He said we could all stay there that night but that was it. "We will help you to evacuate if you have a place to go. We will not take anyone to the Superdome. Enough said about that place. If you don't have anyplace to go we will get you to the Convention Center."

I said to the manager on Thursday morning I was going back to the hospital. I had to find out something definite about my brother. I could not leave without more positive information. I said, "I can't take my luggages with me. I have to leave them here until I get back."

"Remember," Mr. Brown said, "the Marshall wants this place cleared out by noon today."

I asked, "Will you be out by noon?"

He said, "I don't know. I have more paperwork to do and to make sure security has done its job."

I started walking from the hotel but that got too much for me in the brutally hot summer weather. I finally waved a taxi. With all kinds of obstructions and some hours later we finally got to the hospital. The place was completely boarded up. I was so overwhelmed by grief I collapsed at the front door of the hospital. The cab driver said, "Lady, let me try and find some kind of medical service that can give you some help."

"No," I said, "Please, take me back to the hotel."

At the hotel, the driver said to Mr. Brown, "We can't leave her alone and we can't take her to the Superdome or the Convention Center."

Mr. Brown said, "Our liability would be too great. I will be here late tonight and our workers and security people will be here till morning. Let me check with the housekeeper just to be on the safe side." When he came back he said, "She can stay here tonight." The cab driver said he could be here in the morning to take me to the Center. The manager said, "No, I want to make sure she is able to travel. The hotel doesn't need to incur any additional liabilities." Mr. Brown said, "Lady, you are good to stay tonight but you have to leave Friday before noon. I will have one of the females keep checking on you all night. If you need help give her a call- she will be in the next room."

The cab driver was very nice. He gave me his card and said, "If you need anything, please give me a call." I thanked him and we talked just a little bit and he went on his way.

One of the housekeepers came with me to my room. I said to her, "Since my collapse I have been a little unsettled but I think I will be alright."

The lady said, "If you want me to stay I will."

"No, I will be okay." After she left I began to worry whether I would ever see my brother again. What was I going to do? I wanted my brother home whether he is living or deceased. I wanted him home. In a very forceful way it dawned upon me that the hospital gave me a complete run-around. There was something wrong over there. Yes, the whole thing over there seemed to me like some big cover-up.

I had a worrisome night's sleep and when I came down Mr. Brown was having coffee. He said, "Please sit down, I will make you a cup. There is an article in the paper about the hospital your brother was in." He said, "The article states just before the hurricane came Monday morning the entire staff abandoned the hospital and all of its patients. All of the patients drowned. The article says there is some doubt if all of the bodies can be recovered."

By this time the cab driver came with the news. The manager asked him to join us. "We are discussing the article."

The driver said, "When I left here yesterday I went back over there. I knew something was not right when we were over there the other day. I did not say anything to you because you were already upset. So I went back yesterday. The guard and the attendant would not give me, or any of the other people who had gathered there, any information. Then I saw the article this morning- that is the reason I came back to see how you are making out."

I said to him, "He was my brother. What am I going to do? I beg, what am I to do?" Every time I went to the hospital my fears that something was deeply wrong grew bigger and bigger. The sad truth, which I never wanted to admit, now could not be denied. My only brother, my closest kin, was now gone forever.

Mr. Brown said, "I will get her to the Center as agreed." After this news I just received I asked the manager if I could go upstairs for a few minutes to compose myself. He said, "Yes." I took the article with me. He said a worker would be up to check on me in a short time. I thanked the manager and said goodbye to the cab driver.

A lady came up some time later and said, "It is time to get you over to the Center." When we arrived at the Center the manager and I talked for a few minutes. He asked if I was alright and what was I going to do?

"I will try to contact relatives. As for my brother I will live with the hope that some day I can get his body home for a decent burial. Our family has been buried in this same cemetery since before the War Between the States. I want my brother there. I don't know what is really going to happen- I will just leave our fate to the way it has always been- to the will of the Lord. Mr. Brown you have been very kind and I will carry your kindness with me always." He accepted my good will gesture and we gratefully departed.

"I came to the Center," Ms. Prevost said, "and to my good fortune I met those six young ladies you saw me with before. They took care of me last night and today. Those ladies said they would stay with me until a group was found I could stay with. As all of you noticed when they were leaving we hugged and cried as if they were my own grandchildren. I was sorry to see them go. It is a shame we had to part. They are being sent to New Mexico. What day is it?"

Phil said, "It is Saturday, September 3rd."

A young lady said, "They are calling us out- we are on our way to Houston. We have to go."

Someone said, "Looks like the group is down to just a few of you."

We said, "Yes, it looks that way." We shook hands and some of them embraced as security led them to the processing center. Security called the next number and everyone said their goodbyes and as they went through the gate, a couple of them said, "Looks like you two are the last ones in our group."

I said, "Yes, we are the group," as they turned and walked away. There were some pleasant short conversations between Ms. Prevost and me. Our numbers were finally called. We too went through the processing center. I went under the close scrutiny of the security guards. Ms. Prevost asked if I would stay until she finished the process. I said I would, no problem at all.

She said, "Thank you."

Ms. Prevost said she had relatives in St. Louis and Atlanta and she gave their contact information to the associate. She said it didn't matter which one was contacted- she could stay with either of them. The associate said, "This could take some time."

When the associate returned she said, "We have made contact with your family in Atlanta. Come with me and you can talk with them. I will confirm the travel plans while you are on the phone." The associate said, "We will get you to the San Antonio airport. There will be a plane leaving for Atlanta not too long after you arrive. Just take it easy- it will be five or ten minutes before the shuttle gets her."

The shuttle arrived just about on time. I was talking to some staff members when Ms. Prevost walked up to me and said, "Goodbye." She took a step back and paused for a few heartbeats. The staff looked at her. When she took a step forward she said, "Mister, I have never in my life hugged a colored boy before. Please let me hug you." I said yes. We hugged. She said, "Thank you," and politely walked toward the shuttle bus.

I was smiling as the staff members looked stunned. One of them took a good look at me and said, "How could you let that old white woman call you a boy, and you are standing here grinning?"

"I don't know." I walked into the manager's office, closing the door behind me.

XXXIX

The Endless Journey

The manager said, "Before we get you over to the Windsor Ward, I would like to talk to you about our plans for Kelly. My name is Wagner, by the way. It has been decided by the higher ups we are going to keep Kelly as the main hurricane evacuation center. With all these people relocating here there will be a lot of social activities we will have to put together. I heard you talking to my associate about your theatre and art things you used to do out there in Hollywood. We will need some help to put any kind of program together. You can see in that big room we have tons of books and things. We will need some kind of library." He said, "We will have to do something for these kids. There are too many of them here already with nothing to do. I am telling you this because the officer in charge asked me to be on the lookout for someone who could help us put this whole thing in shape. I could talk with him Monday morning and we could have somebody come pick you up at Ward. We could see how this thing could be worked out. That is, if you are at all interested."

"Yes," I said.

He said, "I will call the shuttle and get you over to Windsor. The large group has already gone, but you should be there just in time for the orientation. As we get this thing worked out you will have to move back to Kelly, you know, so don't get too comfortable over there."

The session at Windsor was jammed with evacuees from all over the city. I knew a good many of them. Officer Stanley talked for about a half an hour or less on how well the evacuation process was organized and carried out. He stated how proud he was of the men and women who participated in this effort. It appeared some of the people were uneasy with these remarks since they had a different take on how the process was carried out. Al said to me, "What in the hell this man is talking about?"

Officer Stanley realized he did not hit a home run with these people. He said, "Let me make this clear and very clear. No one will be relocated back to New Orleans until the emergency evacuation order is lifted. Since we are all still in the throes of the hurricane season, who knows how long you folks will have to be with us. We at Windsor will make every effort to make your stay a reasonable one. However," Officer Stanley said, "Let me inform each and every one of you that Windsor Ward Park is a family community. We expect you to respect our laws and the families of this community. In case you have any concerns you may contact any number of our officers who will be patrolling or posted in and about the Park. In the past we have experienced some confusion on the part of some evacuees, particularly from the New Orleans area, understanding the laws of San Antonio, Texas. If there are any infractions of the laws the responsible person or persons will be brought to justice in the San Antonio court system." He said, "Everyone understands me so far? Good. Let me sum this up. This is very important to everybody." Officer Stanley said, "Folks, you are in Texas and you will be governed under the laws of Texas, not the laws of New Orleans. I want to say one last thing. Welcome to San Antonio, Texas. It is a pleasure to have you folks at Windsor Ward Park. Goodnight," he said.

My thing was to check out the place- after all, the man said we were going to be here for a while. That sounds like home to me. I wanted to talk to a few friends to get a little feedback on the lecture we just had a short time ago and if there was any news from the Convention Center before it got too late. There must be a thousand or more evacuees at Ward and many more were trickling in. Groups were everywhere. The place was buzzing with angry conversations. Some friends were upset at the way in which these officers handled the meeting. Dan said, "The officer gave us so little respect, the whole thing was degrading. The man took a very condescending attitude from the very beginning and we had to sit there and take his shit. What else could we do? They had us where they wanted us and he insulted us all."

Roy said, "It's the same old stuff over and over again everywhere we go."

"It looks like we ain't never gonna get rid of the bullshit," Mel said. "We have to put another group together like we had at the Superdome. When we went in and talked to the man we got something done. We have to get the group moving first thing in the morning. If not we will be in his office first thing Monday morning. We got to talk to them about the military guards on one side of us and the police on the other side. What in the hell are we supposed to be, a bunch of criminals or something?"

Earl said, "I bet you that's what they all think. We are a bunch of criminals or something." Many people in the group agreed with that assessment.

Roy said, "Those people in charge are going to talk to us or we gonna take to the streets."

After I was introduced to everybody I said, "Marching is a very real tool to have- don't let them take it away. It is getting late," I said. "I have to move on."

They said, "We heard you, man."

On my way back to my sleeping area I was beckoned by some friends I knew from the Center. Isaac said, "We need to put several groups together so we can really talk to these people."

Louis said, "We have been here for a couple days. FEMA has been doing their whatever and they have not said anything to us. The Red Cross has been better, like feeding us and with medical supplies and all that kind of stuff. The Cross said they would have the long distance lines set up early next week. What else we got, I don't know," he said.

Isaac said, "We must have an expense-free guaranteed Right of Return. And when and how do they plan to get us back home to New Orleans? These are the things," he said, "we need these people to answer for us. And we got to get some answers. What do you think?"

I said, "So many of the folks you have in the groups are good people. They all have been around about a week. They know what to do. If the group can stick to what it needs, it will no doubt accomplish what it wants."

He said, "I gonna let you go, you look beat."

I said, "Yes, I am."

He said, "One thing has been rolling around in my mind." He went on to say, "These people have been shipping us Black people all over the country. And maybe elsewhere, I can't say for sure. Do you think we will ever get back home? I mean our homes in New Orleans?"

Before I could come up with my best answer, Jonas said, "They didn't ship us out to ship us back. Smitty," he said, "When you are gone you are gone and that's your home now. There ain't no coming back."

Isaac said, "Hey man, cut us some slack," as Jonas walked away. Isaac continued, "Looks like we have about twenty-five bodies or more who would like to hear what you have to say. So why don't we pull some of these tables and chairs together and have a good sit down before you start talking." He said, "I don't think we will upset any of those people over there. Anyway, with all of those army guards outside and those local cops trampling up and down this place they won't let us get anywhere near out of hand. Man, everybody in here can see they got us under wraps." Isaac said, "Smitty, it's all yours. Just be real with us, that's all we're asking."

I began. "Thanks everybody. It looks to me like some of you folks are still a little upset. Early on I had a few words with Roy, Dan and Earl and a few others who had a little rough time with the speaker. Folks, we have such large problems slapping us in our faces we gonna have to turn some of these small hurts a loose, man, let them go. Well it looks like a few of us have finally made it to high ground. Isaac, like so many people here, I think the people at the Center would tend to agree with what Jonas had to say. You know, the coming home deal was the constant talk over there. Well folks, here is my take on why the government will never give all of us an expense-free Right of Return to our homes.

"Isaac, I don't think your concerns can properly be addressed by focusing all of the attention only on our present set of circumstances. Don't you think if we looked at some aspects of the history of our relationship with the Rulers of the Empire we could possibly arrive at a more concrete understanding of what this government's hidden agenda may well hold for us? I would think so, as do others.

"We all know, without a doubt, the American experience has wreaked upon us many harsh and painful judgments. In spite of the brutal treatment, we have many of our brothers and sisters who would prefer the memories of those agonizing episodes be buried in the plow fields alongside our distant forbearers. We must accept the fact that our history is our history, however unpleasant it may be. And take that long, hard, painful look at our relationship with the Master of the Empire. The deeper we probe, I am sure the clearer our vision will become of what devious plans the masters had concocted against us.

Without such an understanding, we are mere co-conspirators in a vain pursuit of our freedom.

"It appears to a lot of us, in the beginning when the white man snatched us out of Africa he never intended for us to ever have, as our own, life, liberty and the pursuit of happiness. If we check out the mindset of the masters during that period we can easily see the reasoning for their actions. The white man for centuries prior to the African invasion dreamed of a slave empire.

"When the Church decreed the people of sub-Saharan Africa were uncivilized, and in fact heathens, that introduced color into that diabolical scheme of slavery. Color opened the floodgates to the largest and continuous theft of human beings in the history of humankind. Europe and America declared an economic war on the helpless people of southern Africa, as the world watched the great empires of the north deconstruct the kingdoms of the south.

"Let me continue. The reality of the north-south American slave empire, which would dwarf the great Greek and Roman slave states, was now under construction. When slavery was proclaimed the linchpin of the empire it was also announced slavery was forever. The masters have always been in the relentless pursuit of an expanding empire with endless profits. Slavery was the stock and trade upon which the Empire expanded and the never-ending profits were made. Folks, we have always been shipped out with our broken families, at any time, by any means, to any place they wanted to ship us, at the whims of the masters.

"Isaac, let me offer you and the group my final take on this matter from which each of you can draw your own conclusions and take your own path to wherever. I think we have always been denied the right to participate in this American Experience, which suggests to any reasonable person that we have always been on the outside of the democratic process. Consequently, if we take our present situation, I believe there will be a very large body of Black people who will never again return to New Orleans. Not in this lifetime. When you are gone you are gone forever."

Isaac said, "Smitty, I want to thank you.

Louis said, "We all want to thank you, man."

I said, "Thanks everybody, and it's time to move on."

It was good to be cleaned up and settled in on my cot with my bag under my head. I was not yet ready for a pillow. I had my backpack between my legs as usual for safety. Of course, I missed my blanket, but I guess I didn't really need it any more. They gave me a brand new sheet. As I laid back, I pulled the sheet up over me out of habit.

High up on the wall the faded letters of an honored glory long since gone had been plastered over several times and were barely visible to the naked eye. "Welcome to Montgomery Ward in the Mall," the sign read as the lights faded to black on this Endless Journey.

It was time to move on.

So many evacuees expressed the idea that the authorities were shipping us from here to there and everywhere, to places we had never been, and that we would never return to our homes. The evacuees claimed the Ruling Class was serious about carrying out its plan and they were frightened just trying to save their lives and make it back to New Orleans. Many people advanced the notion that the way in which the plan was carried out, it had to be an outgrowth of some political design.

One of the most unusual groups we encountered advanced the idea that, since we are now non-persons, we will forever be systematically excluded, by whatever means, from full participation in this present paradigm of democracy.

Despite our persistent pursuit of this American Dream, it remains, even for the best of Black people, but a myth.

Our dreams, like our history, must be ours to follow diligently to fulfill our destiny.

After graduating from Xavier University, Smitty settled in Chicago. He was the Assistant Manager in the Credit and Collection Department at Provident Hospital. And shortly became Administrative Assistant to the President of United Transport Service Employees: AFL-CIO. Like many other small unions, U.T.S.E. was an entirely African American labor union. Smitty also tried law school for a while.

In California, Smitty worked as an Internal Revenue Agent in the IRS for several years. Subsequently he opened the legendary Epicurian Coffeehouse on Sunset Blvd, and later the Déjà vu Coffeehouse Gallery, the longest running coffeehouse in LA. In addition he opened the Fifth Estate and the Seventeen-o-Nine Theatres. Smitty received the Los Angeles Drama Critic Circle Award for his theatrical contributions to theatre and the arts.

In 1994, Smitty opened Media tape International, a tape and CD duplication business.

In 2004 he relocated back to New Orleans.

ACKNOWLEDGEMENTS

I am grateful to the many people who have helped to keep the journey alive. Some few are mentioned below.

- Gordon Stith & Frank Mendoza
  Hippies from the 60's

- Bob Meola & Robert Leventer
  Political activists from the 70's

- Denis Alvino & Carl Orsini
  Friends from the coffeehouse of the 70's

- Elaine Suranie & Georgeanne Bartylak
  Theatre colleagues from the 80's

- Eloise & Geraldine Amos, Vera Frezell
  Of long ago

- Mack McClendon at the Lower 9th Ward Village, Tom Pepper at Common Ground Relief, and to all people associated with each.

A very special thank you to my brother, Wilfred, and cousins, Lawrence and Rose.

Dedicated to the cause, took charge the very first moment. Her persistent directions kept me and the project on the straight and narrow. Without her kind of guidance, this endeavor would have long ago come to naught.

As usual, time slips away, all things will fade, yet nothing ceases to be.

Thankfully, in the dreams of make believe, nothing is haplessly beyond recall in our dreams within the dream.

15605101R00149

Made in the USA
Charleston, SC
11 November 2012